"Doris Colgate knows what women want. Well-known as a sailing role model and a confident yet gentle teacher, she writes with clarity on even the most complex sailing concepts, as well as answering often-asked questions on the safety, comfort, and social sides of sailing. *Sailing: A Woman's Guide* pulls it all together for the beginning sailor. Finally, an excellent book for women that both teaches and motivates. Bravo, Doris. You've opened up the sport."

—Bernadete Bernon, editorial director, *Cruising World*

"It took a person with her fingers to the pulse of women aspiring to sail to write this book, and that person is clearly Doris Colgate. *Sailing: A Woman's Guide* is as much a source book as empowerment to women the world over desiring to become sailors."

—Micca Leffingwell Hutchins, editor of SailNet

"An excellent introduction to the sport of sailing. It will undoubtedly encourage many women to try this challenging, noncontact activity while enjoying the great outdoors."

—Betsy Alison, four-time Rolex Yachtswoman of the Year

"This new series is designed to teach outdoor skills to women in the way they learn. . . . Women of all ages describe how they overcame obstacles, what they enjoyed most, or just how they felt about undertaking a new activity . . . extremely well done and appealing."

—*Library Journal* [starred review]

Ragged Mountain Press Woman's Guides—the first book series for the growing number of women who are active outdoors.

A Ragged Mountain Press
WOMAN'S GUIDE

SAILING

DORIS COLGATE

Series Editor, Molly Mulhern Gross

RAGGED MOUNTAIN PRESS / McGRAW-HILL
Camden, Maine • New York • San Francisco • Washington, D.C. • Auckland • Bogotá
Caracas • Lisbon • London • Madrid • Mexico City • Milan • Montreal
New Delhi • San Juan • Singapore • Sydney • Tokyo • Toronto

CONTENTS

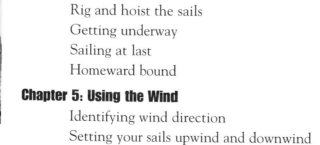

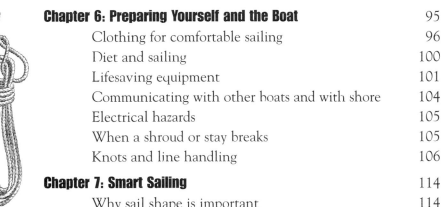

CONTENTS

Acknowledgments

This book is inspired by my peers and the thousands of women I have met through courses at Offshore Sailing School, at "Take the Helm" seminars for women, and on the water cruising and racing. I am moved by their enthusiasm, their constant search for more knowledge and sailing confidence, and their desire to learn from women sailors who've "been there."

In preparing this book, I sent mammoth questionnaires to two groups of women: to sixty women who teach sailing at schools across the country, and to a thousand women who went to sailing school. The tips and experiences of the experts are mixed in these pages with the candid remarks and insights of students. I thank them all for giving so freely to this project.

I am particularly grateful to Offshore Sailing School Operations Manager Michelle Boggs, for sharing her many teaching tips and methods; to the founding board of the National Women's Sailing Association—Marcia Andrews, Lyn Fontanella, Kate Kerr, and Diana Smith—for standing with me these many years in our mission to enrich women's lives through education and access to sailing; to Marcia Andrews, Cynthia Flanagan Goss and Kathryn Mallien for their invaluable efforts in editing this book; to the vision of Molly Mulhern Gross, for making this series come about; and to my nonsailor father Bernie Horecker, for taking the time to comment on the original manuscript from stem to stern.

There is one person who stands out above all others as the true inspiration behind my career in sailing. I am forever indebted to my husband, Steve Colgate, for sharing his love of sailing for more than thirty years and for encouraging me to write this book. He is the reason for my success, and for the many changing horizons in this passion we live and love.

When I began to write this book, the women I talked with said, "Wow, that's great. Finally someone is talking to us!" These women thought such a book would have accelerated their learning curves. I, for one, am sure it would have helped me. I believe women have issues that seldom get expressed, ways of learning about sailing that are different, and special motivations that benefit from encouragement and openness.

More and more women are getting into sailing. It's time to confront old notions that sailing is a male-dominated sport, too expensive, too hard, too scary, and too time consuming. Sailing is what you want it to be. I've heard all the bravado—stories about crossing storm-tossed seas, pushing boat and body to their limits. But that's not what I wanted from sailing. I wanted to try something new—a sport that mixed a little challenge with a lot of peaceful rewards. I wanted to take the helm of a sailboat and feel it react to my touch, glide silently through calm waters, and relish the excitement of wind-whipped spray on my face. I wanted to see the world under sail.

THE MANY REWARDS OF SAILING

The sea must not be taken lightly, and blind trust should not be instilled in every sailor and sailboat. A mentor once told me, "The sea can be most unforgiving at times." True. But the sea and the lakes and rivers you sail on can also provide the most spectacular life experiences.

Sailing is an activity that lasts a lifetime. You can sail on a shoestring or in grand luxury, with as little or as much financial commitment as you can afford or desire. Sailing is an activity to share with your friends, your partner, your husband and kids—or to enjoy alone. It is a lot easier to master than golf, not nearly as scary as white-water rafting, and far more forgiving than flying. Each sailing experience is a little different, and each has its own special sense of accomplishment. You can wipe away a stressful day with a sunset sail, get away for an hour on a nearby lake, drive to the shore for a weeklong cruise with family or friends, or sign on as crew for a weekend sailing regatta. You can even cash it all in and set sail—for a month, a year, or maybe forever.

I believe sailing has added years to my life. A special kind of relaxation comes over me when I leave the dock. When I'm racing, a healthy burst of adrenaline clears my mind for whatever challenge lies ahead. There are no boundaries: the world is your playground, the sea and the rivers are your roadways, and the horizon is always changing. This is what I love about sailing.

WHAT IS SAILING?

My simple definition of sailing is moving a boat through the water by means of wind alone: no engines, no paddles; just the wind in your sails.

Centuries ago, aside from rowing, sailing was the only way to cross bodies of water and travel from island to island or from continent to continent. Fishermen and whalers went to sea in large schooners, and from their mother ship, they launched small dories each day to find their quarry. Much of the world was discovered under sail. Men like Columbus and Magellan steered by the stars and charted the waters we sail on today.

Later, sailing was also done for sport. In 1851, the sailing yacht *America* won the Hundred Guineas Cup around Britain's Isle of Wight. In the 1930s, elegant J-Class yachts over a hundred feet long with towering masts were campaigned in races off English and American shores and across the ocean by Liptons, Vanderbilts, and their friends and foes.

Some incredible sailing yachts have been owned by women. Barbara Hutton's glamorous schooner *Sea Cloud* is still sailing today. It was known for its marble fireplaces, stately library and piano, imperious grand saloon, and elegant guest rooms. The owners of these grand yachts had little sailing dinghies too, and they enjoyed friendly competition for solid silver trophies in East Coast harbors.

Gradually, sailing spread to our lakes and rivers and across the country to the West Coast. It became affordable and accessible. Today, with a little training, you can try sailing off a resort beach or in a city park. There are thousands of schools scattered across the country in nearly every state. Once you're hooked the options are endless.

A sailboat can be a 13-foot dinghy you sail alone or a 100-foot schooner, with many options in between. You don't have to own a sailboat to be a sailor. You can rent one for an hour, a day, a weekend, a week or more. And you can do this just about anywhere there's a body of water. More and more sailing clubs are springing up in metropolitan areas. Singles and couples find these especially convenient, for they can sail anytime they want with other club members or friends.

The only limits to your sailing are determined by your desire and your skill level. If you want to go along and sail with others, you can get by with minimal knowledge. But if you want to rent or charter a boat yourself, you need to know how to handle that type of boat. Which would you choose? If you're like me, you'll choose to be a sailor in your own right.

ABOUT THIS BOOK

This book is for women who are new to sailing and also for women sailors who want to build their skills and develop confidence in their abilities. At first, sailing may seem complicated and very challenging. But each step of the short, initial learning process takes you closer to the ultimate reward: that supreme sense of accomplishment when you set sail alone for the first time.

Do women approach learning to sail differently from men? I think so. "Men are from Mars and women are from Venus; we sure do things differently!" says Stephanie Argyris, a one-time sailing student who is now a certified sailing instructor. In my experience, women want to know what they're getting into before they try something new: They want to learn skills on shore and understand the technique before they try them on the water. Knowing how to perform the basic skills of sailing isn't enough. Most women want to know the whys, so they can act logically when the need arises.

In this book, you'll learn the hows and the whys, and you'll learn how other women approached sailing. I'll tell you how to get started, where to learn, and what to look for in a sailing school. I'll tell you how to prepare for going sailing, what to wear, and how to make yourself comfortable on a boat. I'll tell you about weather and how to handle emergencies. By the time you finish this book, you'll understand the techniques you need to set sail and return safely on your own. I'll tell you how you can continue sailing once you've mastered the basics and what sailing can do for you and your kids.

You'll meet women in this book whose lives have been changed by sailing, others who live for sailing, and others who count sailing among the many activities they do. Experts and novices and racers and cruisers alike all share their insights.

A sailor never stops learning, and each moment on the water adds to her personal gratification. The more you sail, the more you want to share it with others who don't. That's the beauty of sailing.

Chapter 1

⛵ WOMEN AND SAILING

I am lying awake in the cockpit, gazing up at a jet-black sky filled with stars. Suddenly, a light darts across. Then another. Shooting stars! The universe is so big, and we are so small as we bob along on the dark sea. I feel secure yet elated—eager to see what dawn will bring. It's my turn to steer, my turn to feel the gentle roll of the sea as our 60-foot ketch adjusts to my touch. I'm on the helm, guiding us silently through the Anegada Passage in the British Virgin Islands, watching the compass and the slivers of moonlight that glint on the horizon. I'm comfortable and confident, sailing not as a passenger but as one of a team that makes decisions and shares responsibilities. I'm on the lead sailboat in a flotilla with graduates of Offshore Sailing School. This is my life now.

I remember my first exposure to sailing. It was a Monday, my first day as a secretary at *Yachting* magazine in New York City. The company's small, congenial staff was all abuzz about their weekend sailing. Some sailed with their kids in club regattas, others poked around nearby harbors with friends, others competed in their local summer racing series. My boss had just finished a cruise along the coast of Maine, and the managing editor, Marcia Wiley, spent the weekend sailing with friends on the Chesapeake. They were all tanned and relaxed, curiously happy on a summer Monday at work. I had to be part of this scene. I asked Marcia, who soon became my inspiration and mentor, where I could learn to sail. With her advice, I embarked on a totally new lifestyle.

• •

"**A**ny woman who can drive in Boston, New York, or Paris can learn to maneuver through any harbor in the world. Any woman who can run a PC, fax, or VCR can operate a loran or GPS. Any woman who can manage a half-dozen twelve-year-olds at a circus can organize a crew, but—and this is the crucial point—only if she wants to."

—Sheila McCurdy Brown, age 45

• •

After taking a course at Offshore Sailing School thirty-two years ago, I not only fell in love with sailing: I fell in love with the school's owner and eventually married them both. Since then I've been passionate about women and sailing. I pushed our company to provide more opportunities for women, and I started an advisory board to introduce more women to sailing.

There were still more men than women taking up sailing in those early days, but the women were memorable. Some were just coming off divorces, others were recently widowed, and some came with partners to learn more together about the sport. Some were just returning to the work field, but most were (and still are) independent career women intent on mastering new skills and eager to enjoy the personal rewards and camaraderie of sailing.

Now I organize seminars and create programs to help women build confidence in themselves and have more fun sailing. When I'm not sailing, I long for those quiet days cruising in crystal waters—deep in my own thoughts, the wind in my hair, the sun on my back. Sailing changed my life. It can change yours. I hope this book will not only inspire you to try sailing but accelerate your learning curve and give you a reassuring start to a lifetime of sailing pleasure.

A GREAT FIT FOR WOMEN

A skilled sailor needs a sense of awareness and anticipation, ability to concentrate, and sensitivity to her surroundings. I find women can see, hear, and absorb several things at once, yet still focus on the job at hand. In my experience, women are good communicators, good team players, supportive, helpful, understanding, and willing to listen and talk about what's bothering them. These qualities make women very good sailors.

There are no real barriers for women learning to sail. Supreme strength and agility are not required for sailing. Deck gear utilizes pulleys and winches to give sailing crews a mechanical advantage. "A woman who wants to sail can use mechanical advantages at any age," says 75-year old instructor Betty Pearce. And sailboats don't know the gender of the person helming or working the sails!

WHY ARE WOMEN DRAWN TO SAILING?

Sailing is many things to many different women. Sailing can represent freedom, fun, tranquillity, a physical challenge, or a chance to be close to nature. Some women are drawn to the pace of a long cruise; these women cruisers radiate gentle-ness, courage, and self-assurance. Other women seek the challenge of competition: They're stimu-lated by reaching a personal best and strengthened by working in a well-honed crew. Sailing offers each woman her own unique rewards.

> "**S**ailing is very relaxing: When I'm sailing, I'm inaccessible."
>
> —Denise Theri, age 49

For Jean, a gentle breeze and solitude is all that matters. She keeps a 100-pound, 12-foot boat called a Byte in her garage. When she gets home from work, she throws it on her roof rack. In ten minutes, she's sailing on her own on a nearby pond.

Sue loves to sail where the weather is always warm, trade winds blow, and romantic coves beckon—so her goal was to become skilled enough to skipper a sailboat in the Caribbean. She doesn't want to own a boat, but her perfect getaway is a Caribbean charter, reaching along the shore of a palm tree-lined island with good friends at her side.

For Dinah, sailing offered a chance to explore. She keeps her 20-footer in Maine and spends her summers poking around its magical coves. Sometimes she takes friends; other times she sails alone. Her joy is navigating deserted inlets, or ghosting along in an eerie fog with a familiar buoy clanging in the distance. When the day is over, she'll curl up below in her cozy cabin and read herself to sleep as gentle waves lap the hull of her boat.

For Ellie, who shares sailing with her family on a 35-footer in Chesapeake Bay, the greatest pleasure is seeing her 8-year-old son help his dad trim the sails and watching her 12-year-old daughter bring the boat smartly into its slip. Sailing gives Ellie and her family the chance to work as a team.

> "**A** whole new world of travel and adventure has opened for me through sailing."
>
> —Linda White, age 58

Kim loves the heat of competition. When she isn't racing her own boat, she'll hop aboard a friend's 24-footer as crew. It's exhilarating for her to see a colorful spinnaker pop open as it fills with wind, or to feel her boat speed forward as she fights for the lead. High fives and a cold beer at the local watering hole are the perfect finale for a satisfying day on the water.

WOMEN WHO SAIL

Stephanie Argyris started sailing in diapers with her mom and dad. When she was seven years old, her mother died. After that, her dad took Stephanie and her younger brother sailing on summer weekends in his 15-foot Sneakbox. As a young woman, Stephanie pursued a career in medicine, becoming a physician who specializes in rehabilitative medicine, and she dabbled with flying hot air balloons. Twenty years passed. She moved back to the shores of Barnegat Bay, and there she restored her dad's beloved eighty-year-old boat. In her forties, she decided to take a sailing course to improve her skills. Five years ago, she founded Sail-Habilitation—a not-for-profit organization that provides sailing lessons for people with physical disabilities and other

• •

"**W**omen have natural ability on the water. They're good at finding wind; they take a common sense approach to a challenge and solve it. Then they relax and enjoy its beauty."

—Micca Hutchins, age 52

• •

impairments. She can now help others return to as normal a life as possible after catastrophic injury and give her patients the experience of a lifetime.

Sailing became part of Stephanie's spirit and soul—and she found a way to integrate it into her life in a meaningful way. The women in this gallery of profiles have done the same, each in their own unique way.

Cruising women

Some sailing women have traded life on land for life on a boat. Lin Pardey walked away from a management career and onto a sailboat in her early twenties. "Sailing looked like a way to meet clean-living people," she explains. "I had $200, and I wanted to leave the California desert and buy a sailboat." She went down to the docks and met Larry, a professional sailor and charter captain. Three days later, they ran away to sea together. The Pardeys have been together thirty-two years: cruising 154,000 miles, writing ten books, giving seminars in twelve different countries. "Sailing is magic," says the 4-foot, 10-inch 54-year-old. They live and cruise on the 29-foot teak and bronze boat they built themselves, with fittings and gear positioned for Lin's height and strength, a luxurious lounge, bathtub, heater, big oven, fine dishes and crystal wine glasses, an ice chest that lasts fifteen to eighteen days in the tropics, and a stereo. The boat has no engine and minimal electronics. Lin is focused on encouraging women to enjoy the simplicity of sailing and do everything possible to keep gaining ability.

Mel Neale, age 52, lives aboard a 47-footer with her husband, Tom, and two daughters, Melanie and Caroline. An accomplished sailor, photographer, and artist, Mel convinced her successful but stressed hus-

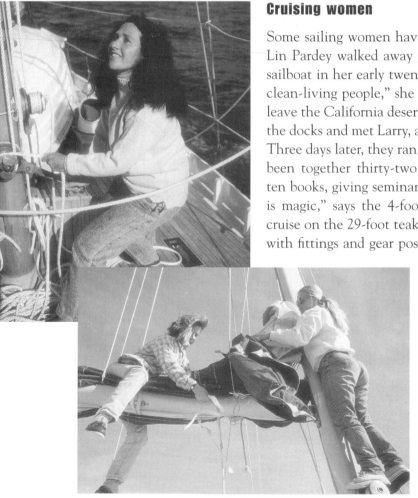

Top: Lin Pardey at the mast of her own boat. **Bottom:** Melanie and Caroline Neale aboard *Chez Nous.*

• •

"I love feeling the wind, hearing
the silence."

—Jane Candella, age 49

• •

Barbara Marrett on an ocean crossing.

band to trade in a thriving law career for sailing. It wasn't hard. The girls (19 and 17) have lived aboard since birth. Their backyard stretches along the East Coast—from Newport, Rhode Island, in the summer to the Bahamas in the winter. Home-schooled and delightfully composed, with rosy skin and sun-streaked hair, they join their parents in spreading the word about cruising.

Barbara Marrett is a tall, slim blonde in her mid-forties with a special beauty that speaks of distant places and treasured experiences. She embarked on sailing eleven years ago when she agreed to sail with her fiancé to Easter Island. She didn't know where the island was, and she knew nothing about sailboats and sailing. They cruised 45,000 miles in three years—as far north as Alaska and as far south as New Zealand. The people they met along the way changed her life forever.

On her own now, Barbara has reexamined sailing: "Until a woman gets on a boat as a captain, without anyone to second-guess her, she can't really gain confidence. It's too easy to avoid taking responsibility." Now West Coast contributing editor for *Cruising World* magazine, Barbara has coauthored two books, and she lectures and inspires women to open their lives to the sensations of sailing. Through sailing, she says, "many of us have learned to value time over money, people over possessions, serenity over status."

Competitors

Of the women who embrace the helm in the 1990s, 34-year-old Dawn Riley takes center stage. She is the only woman in the world who has completed two grueling Whitbread Round-the-World Races and competed in two America's Cup campaigns. In 1994, she was captain of the all-women Whitbread *Heineken* team (which she wrote about in her book, *Taking the Helm*), and in 1995, she was team captain of the all-women *Mighty Mary* America's Cup team. Now CEO of America True: The San Francisco Challenge, she's the first woman to head an America's Cup effort. She is determined to win the Cup back for the United States in the year 2000 with the only truly coed team.

In 1997, the International Olympic Committee mandated that competitors in all sports be 30 percent women by the 2004 Olympics. One of those intent on going for the gold is Newport

Betsy Alison teaching young sailors.

(Rhode Island) sailor Betsy Alison. At 37, she's the only four-time recipient of the Rolex Yachtswoman of the Year award. In 1997, she won her fifth International Women's Keelboat Championship, and in 1998 she took gold and silver medals at the International Sailing Federation World Championships. As comfortable racing with men as she is with women—like so many women who excel in sailing—Betsy holds nothing back in sharing her secrets of success. "The most stupid question is the one you don't ask," she says.

Tough and tenacious Tracy Edwards, 35, skippered the first all-female Whitbread Round-the-World Race entry in 1989. She and her crew on *Maiden Great Britain* finished second in the Maxi class and won two legs of the race along the way. In the winter of 1998, she attempted to win the Jules Verne Trophy for the fastest nonstop global circumnavigation under sail. Tracy's all-women crew of ten abandoned that incredible effort when their 92-foot catamaran *Royal & SunAlliance* crashed into a massive wave and lost its mast in frigid waters about 2,000 nautical miles west of South America. In the January 1998 issue of *Soundings*, Tracy talks about sailing with women. "It's much more comfortable," she says. 'Women are cleaner, tidier, more receptive to each other, care about each other, and don't indulge in a lot of bravado."

Women at the helm

More and more women are not only learning to share the helm equally with male sailing partners, they're going off on their own as boat owners, charter captains, and skippers in their own right. The daughter of a famous marine architect, Sheila McCurdy Brown grew up sailing on Long Island Sound—and she doesn't accept gender bias. When she asked for a berth on a transatlantic race at age 21, the only position offered to her was that of cook. Now in her forties, she's sailed over 50,000 miles on boats from 35 to 120 feet long—as navigator, captain, and, yes, cook. "On a crossing from New York to the Azores, I figured out how to make bread with crushed Alka-Seltzer," she explains. "I had an Irish soda bread recipe but no baking soda, so I improvised. If your crew asks,

●●●

"**U**ntil a woman gets on a boat as a captain, without anyone to second-guess her,
she can't really gain confidence. It's too easy to avoid taking responsibility."

—Barbara Marrett, age 41

●●●

tell them the grainy bits are caraway seeds." An educator and writer, Sheila is equally at home dealing with opinion and technical subjects in sailing.

My mentor Marcia Wiley was managing editor of *Yachting*, the oldest sailing magazine, in the 1960s, and she eventually became its editor. She joined *Yachting* straight out of college and stayed until she retired from work in her seventies—but not from sailing. I spent many boat show hours with Marcia, learning to critique new sailboats from a woman's point of view in an era when men thought pink interiors would please us. Much has changed since those days.

Marcia Wiley on the helm during a flotilla cruise in Greece.

Today, nearly all the major sailing publications in the United States are guided by women. Perhaps the most sensitive to women's needs and issues in sailing is Bernadette Bernon, editorial director for The Sailing Company, which publishes *Cruising World*, *Sailing World*, and *The Sailor's Sourcebook*. Bernadette began sailing in college and actively raced from 1980 to 1990. Six years ago, she introduced a magazine forum to examine sailing women's interests. That forum, she says, was the largest reader-letter generator in *Cruising World*'s history. Women wrote that the attitudes revealed represented how they felt about sailing.

Bernadette understands the tug of sailing. Just before she was to be married, author and commentator William F. Buckley invited her fiancé to sail transatlantic with him for his next book. Departure day was right after their honeymoon, and the voyage would last six weeks. "She's a

sailor," said Buckley. "She understands such things." He was right. "Oh, I didn't hesitate. I told him to go," she said. "I wanted us to have a relationship that supported each other's opportunities. Of course," she added with a smile, "I also knew that I'd be getting points for the rest of my life." Tall, glamorous, tranquil, yet a natural performer who enjoys being on stage, Bernadette gathers the stories of women who live the cruising lifestyle.

Patience Wales, a self-proclaimed water rat and editor of *Sail* magazine, is candidly perceptive and delightfully outspoken. Her one-liners spice the pages of a magazine

Patience Wales in the main cabin during a circumnavigation.

that addresses beginners and advanced sailors in both cruising and racing. Now in her early sixties, Patience began sailing as a young adult. In the 1960s she spent four years circumnavigating the world with boat partners aboard a 42-foot ketch. In the late 1980s she took another sabbatical—a 13-month passage aboard her 51-foot cutter called *Boston Light*. With her three boat partners, Patience has owned a total of six boats. She understands what sailing can do for women.

Sailing's diminutive down-to-earth editor, Micca Hutchins, created the magazine's first all-woman issue in 1985. She grew up sailing and introduced her husband-to-be to a lifestyle that not only helped their relationship but continues to be a family activity with their teenage son and daughter. Micca skippered in four Chicago-to-Mackinac Races and the Trans-Superior Race—

Micca Hutchins at the helm on a race.

setting a record as one of the first women to head an entry in the longest freshwater race in the world. "Sailing is an excellent fit for women," she says. "There are no barriers; they come on board and go straight to what they want to do. Women have natural ability on the water; they're good at finding wind, they take a common sense approach to a challenge and solve it. Then they relax and enjoy its beauty."

The stages of a sailing career

Lydia Bird describes her 20-year sailing career in three eras. First she sailed on other people's boats with a great deal of enthusiasm but not much say. As her skills developed, she took a greater role on boats she didn't own. Now she's a boat owner. More than that, she holds the women's record for the Singlehanded Transpac Race from San Francisco to Kauai, Hawaii. Born in 1954, Lydia has made eight major ocean crossings and covered 40,000 offshore miles under sail. In 1997 she wrote a revealing book about her latest, mostly solitary odyssey—a 5,000-mile voyage from Maryland to Greece across the Atlantic and through the Mediterranean on her 42-footer, *Sonnet*. An emotionally complex and sometimes grueling experience, her diary is laced with introspective poetry and discoveries about herself and the intricacies of relationships when three distinctly different women join her at different times in the journey.

You see, women who sail are just like you and me. Young and not so young—single, wives, mothers, grandmothers, widows, and divorcees. They are women with no desire to become dependent on anyone else, women seeking relationships and friends in an activity they can share. Some started as kids, but most entered the sport after college, kids, and beyond.

• •

"**S**ailing really enhances your life and the way you interact with people. Just do it. Don't impose limitations on yourself."

—Dorothy Mosko, age 35

• •

To enjoy sailing, we need to be in control. Control over how we sail, who we sail with, where we sail, and when we sail. But control depends on competence. The more we know, the more we enjoy. The fastest way to gain knowledge—and ultimately control—is to go to school. It's the smart way to build confidence, even for those who already have some sailing experience.

Sailing is a very social activity. It's exciting, challenging, romantic—yet safe. Sailing is a green sport: a clean, fresh-air activity. Sailing is gender free, age free, and provides lifelong possibilities. And above all, sailing truly allows us to get away.

Chapter 2

HOW TO GET STARTED

"**L**earning to sail was the best experience I've ever had. I learned more about myself than I learned in four years of college."

—Dianne Katherine Crigger, age 42

Once you become a sailor, you are no longer content to lie on the beach and gaze at the beautiful white sails on the horizon. You're at the helm, steering in crystal-clear waters with close friends, sharing the warmth of a summer breeze. No longer do you wonder if you'll ever escape the pressures of day-to-day life. You have the most rewarding escape now: Sailing offers peaceful outings close to home and challenging getaways in faraway places. You have a lifetime of new opportunity. Who knows where the wind will take you next?

CHOOSE A SAILING SCHOOL

The best way to begin is to go to school. If you can't find a good program near home, take a course on your next vacation. In three days to a week, you'll get a basic education. Then you can continue on at a more advanced level or gain experience through daysailing, racing, or cruising—either on your own or with family and friends.

There are literally thousands of sailing schools across the nation. Many are not-for-profit community sailing programs that teach on small boats at modest fees. While this is a good way to get your feet wet, consider getting on the fast track at a school certified by US SAILING, the governing body of the sport.

There are many sources you can turn to to find a school in your area. Some schools advertise in the pages of sailing magazines. Some attend boat shows; these shows are a good way to learn about the school's programs and talk to a staff member. Several organizations also publish directories of sailing schools (see the resources chapter, page 165).

Here are questions you should ask before signing up for a course.

- **How are instructors trained and certified?** Look for schools that test their candidate instructors both on and off the water and train them either through US SAILING instructor certification or their own high standards. If a school follows its own standards, these should require instructors to have a high level of knowledge and strong teaching and communication skills. Ask to see the school's criteria or talk to an instructor if you need convincing.

- **Does the school offer classroom instruction to reinforce onboard training?** This shows a level of professionalism and increases the learning curve by giving you the theory behind the hands-on techniques.

- **Is student certification with a national authority such as US SAILING available?** Though not mandatory, certification is a valuable tool to prove your capability to yourself and to others.

- **How long are the courses?** There's a lot to learn in sailing. A course that runs less than three days (or 24 hours of instruction) is usually not enough.

- **What training materials does the school provide?** Do you get a textbook in advance to study? Make sure the school has a curriculum, augmented by textbooks that follow the course outline. Ask if you will get any materials in advance to study. There's a lot to learn, so you'll want a head start.

- **What kind of boat will you learn on?** Does it match the skill levels you seek? How well maintained is the school's fleet? You want to learn on a boat that provides performance, stability, safety, and fun, but one that also allows you to advance to higher levels of skill. If your goal is to sail on a boat big enough to take your friends and family, do a little cruising, or even sleep aboard, you might not want to start on something too small (see Chapter 3 for more on different types of boats). You also want to be sure you are learning on boats that are regularly maintained and outfitted for safety. Does the school care enough to ask graduates to evaluate the condition of their boats? Ask about their maintenance schedule. Make sure they carry Coast Guard–required safety equipment for that size and type boat (such as a throwable cushion on medium-sized training boats). Boats should also have anchors, paddles, and comfortable Coast Guard–approved life vests for everyone aboard.

- **What's the ratio of students per instructor?** One instructor to four students on a boat is normal. More students dilute the instructor's efforts.

- **Does the school offer advanced courses to help you reach your sailing goals?** Do they offer opportunities to continue sailing—such as clubs, rentals, charters? Are the school's courses recognized by charter and rental companies? As you progress, it's nice to know you can return to the school and continue up the learning ladder. Graduate opportunities allow you to practice and fine-tune your skills. Many charter and rental companies recognize certain schools' programs as good training for chartering and renting: The ultimate endorsement for any school is a list of charter and rental companies that want your business!

- **Does the school offer a guarantee?** If a school doesn't stand behind its product, you will want to know why.

- **How long has the school been in operation?** Is teaching its primary business? Does it offer programs throughout the year? The sailing school business is often a labor of love, but the schools that operate like a true business endure. If instruction is an adjunct to selling boats or simply an individual's hobby, the program might not have the resources or commitment to back its product.

- **Is the school adequately insured?** Sailing is a safe sport, but accidents can happen. As with skiing instruction, you will probably be asked to sign a waiver before setting out on a boat. If the school doesn't have minimum $1,000,000 liability insurance (more is better) currently in place, there may have been problems or lack of funds in the past.

- **Can you get names of graduates in your area to check the school's reputation?** Sure, you'll probably only get the names of graduates who had a good experience. But you'll cut through the chaff easily if you ask them the questions I covered above.

Women-only courses

Every spring we hold a special "*You Can Sail Escape*" week for women only on Captiva Island, Florida. In the past seven years, several hundred women have chosen this venue—and for a lot of different reasons.

Dorothy Mosko enjoys a typical sailing course.

Kay Deshler took a cruising course with her two teenage sons, but they criticized and put her down throughout the course. She wanted to be sure she could handle the boat if something happened to her husband in an emergency or if he fell overboard. Kay's husband wants to circumnavigate, and he gave her the "*You* Can Sail Escape" as a gift.

Paula Chekemain and Bonnie Gustin, who were both celebrating their fortieth birthdays, received learn-to-sail courses as presents, too. Bonnie's mission was to "figure it out," since she and her husband had just purchased a new sailboat and were not that skilled.

Linda Witzal took a performance sailing course and bought a J/24 that she describes as a "tricky racing boat." She talked three women coworkers she wanted as crew into the "Escape" course at Offshore Sailing School—because she was tired of male crew telling her what to do.

Dell Zanuck tried sailing after her divorce in 1990, and she vows the phrase "Oh, you sail?" is a great pickup line! But she does the picking and choosing now, because she can charter as a skipper and invite her friends along.

Some women are intimidated around men on sailboats, but they become more outgoing and more willing to try something new in women-only venues where cooperative teamwork, helping one another, and spontaneous laughter seem to dramatically boost confidence levels.

Coed courses

The learning environment is a matter of preference, and some women prefer being around men. Learning with women only "isn't the real world," says 33-year-old Breena Daniell, who took a coed learn-to-sail course in 1996. She echoes a sentiment I often hear, that women-only courses

"There's a camaraderie of sisterhood [in all-women courses]: no fear of embarrassment."

—Kim Auburn, age 39

"My daughter and I took sailing courses together, and we agree this was the best family vacation we've ever had!"

—Cathryn Griffith, age 58

are unrealistic unless you plan to sail only with women. And, "Guys are fun to have around," says 66-year-old Dolores Bittleman.

Some accomplished women racers feel it's fine to start out in all-women venues. But at some point, you need to make the switch to coed racing if you want to get ahead in competitive sailing. There are fewer women racing than men, and competition levels are naturally higher in the large coed fleets. Competing in all-women events can lower the level of competition and, ultimately, lessen our desire or ability to improve.

Many coed schools prefer to place couples who live together on separate boats. Some husbands and male friends become protective and domineering, which inhibits a woman's progress. It's like learning to drive, which is not so easy when your husband, boyfriend, or father is the teacher. If this is your situation, tell the school you and your partner want to be taught on separate boats.

Textbooks and testing

"I was afraid I'd hate sailing. But as soon as I took the helm, I loved it!"

—Jane Candella, 49 years old

You should get a good sailing textbook to guide your learning experience. When you put classroom theory into practice on the water, it's amazing how clear the concepts of sailing become. We use texts written by Steve Colgate for each of our courses. Many other schools have adopted these texts or the manuals published by US SAILING.

Testing is important to reinforce the learning process. This requires concentration, stimulates your memory, and creates better understanding. Women who are less prone to ask questions in a coed situation go away with muddled concepts—making the learning process far longer than it needs to be. Taking tests and discussing the answers shortens the process.

Certification

US SAILING is the governing body for the sport of sailing in the United States, and the organization represents our country's interests as a member of the International Sailing Federation. US SAILING's certification program, offered by qualified sailing schools across the country, provides comprehensive manuals, classroom testing, and on-the-water testing for a variety of different skill levels (see the resources chapter, page 165, for more information).

If the school you choose offers certification, I highly recommend you take it. You'll get a logbook and stickers for each skill level you pass, automatically become a member of US SAILING, and have an easier time renting and chartering later on. Best of all, you'll know what areas you excel in and where you need to improve. I've heard couples decide that only one of them needs to be certified (usually the husband), since they'll be sailing together. This is faulty reasoning and fosters the idea that one sailor should be dependent on the other. Certification may involve an extra fee and testing time outside the regular course. But it's worth it.

"I learned more [in sailing school] than I imagined, and I can take the helm now with a great feeling of satisfaction."

—Cathie Heimbach, age 55

WHAT TO EXPECT ON YOUR FIRST DAY

Your first day on the water will be full of information and new sensations. If you feel a little anxious, you're not alone. Go with an open mind, relax, and approach the experience with realistic goals. You're going to make mistakes: That's part of the learning process.

If you've chosen the right school, you'll start with a classroom session that reinforces your lessons on the water. You should also get a list of what to bring and wear (see Chapter 6, "Clothing for Comfortable Sailing," page 96). Wear old clothes you won't mind getting wet. Expect to be tested, so study before and during the course.

On a typical first day at school, you should be given a comfortable life jacket and taught about safety gear and the proper way to get on and off a sailboat. You'll learn how to rig the boat, how to leave and return from a dock or a mooring, and how to perform basic sailing maneuvers that allow you to change the direction of the sailboat using the sails and the tiller or wheel. You should learn to identify where the wind is coming from and take turns trying all crew positions on the boat. Most of all, you'll get the *feel* of sailing.

In a good program, you and your crewmates will do everything yourselves. A good instructor will talk you through maneuvers and ask you to explain why you're doing them, encourage you when you make mistakes, and praise you when you get it right. She'll stand or sit out of the way, but be close enough to take charge if you need help. She'll watch your progress with a keen eye and recognize when you need a break.

At the end of that first day, you might feel overwhelmed. But it will all come together as the course progresses. On your first solo day out, you'll relish the reality of how much you've learned.

NORMAL APPREHENSIONS

It's normal to have questions about your well-being on the water: you're about to try a new activity with many kinds of new sensations. Let's address these up front. Then you can embark with a clear mind and reassurance that learning to sail will be a truly enjoyable experience.

- **"I'm afraid of capsizing."** You don't have to worry about this if you learn and sail on boats that won't capsize. Most schools that teach adults use comfortable, stable sailboats, so don't worry. If in doubt, ask about the boat's characteristics before you get aboard. (This subject is covered in more detail in Chapter 3.)

"We were tested. It made me nervous, but we learned every step of the way."

—Stephanie Argyris, age 47

- **"I'm afraid when the boat heels."** Sailboats are designed so they can heel (or lean) to one side or the other to capture the wind in their sails. Finding this an unfamiliar or scary feeling at first is a natural reaction. *You* can control the angle of heel in many different ways: by changing the direction of the boat with respect to the wind, easing or changing the way the sails are set, reducing the size of your sails, taking your sails down and turning the engine on, and repositioning where you and your crew mates are sitting and where gear and sails are stowed. I'll tell you more about this in later chapters.

- **"I can't swim."** Believe it or not, lots of women who sail can't swim. Unless you usually sail on small dinghies that easily tip over, it's not very likely you'll go in the water. But having said that, I normally recommend all sailors wear a life jacket while on deck on a sailboat. This is particularly important in heavy wind and during times when you are very active, such as when you're racing. I'll talk more about life jackets and other safety equipment in Chapter 6.

- **"What if I fall overboard?"** If you're sailing alone on a small boat or dinghy, chances are you'll fall out sooner or later. But before you go off on your own, you'll learn how to pull yourself back aboard without much trouble. If you're sailing with friends on a larger boat, the chances of falling overboard are slim. However, before you get aboard, make sure your crewmates know at least one crew-overboard recovery procedure and have proper safety equipment for such emergencies. You'll learn two quick and efficient techniques for recovering someone from the water in Chapter 5 (see "Crew Overboard Recovery," page 90). You should practice these maneuvers over and over.

- **"What if my partner falls overboard and I'm left alone on the boat?"** This is the fear most often expressed by women contemplating sailing with just one other person (usually their spouse). Thousands of couples cruise together every year and very few overboard incidents occur, even in the worst conditions. It's clearly much harder for one person to sail a boat and try to recover someone without help. But it can—and has—been done. Learn the recovery procedures in Chapter 5 and practice with your partner whenever you can.

- **"I'm afraid I'll look like a fool and hate sailing."** You won't have time to worry about how you look: There's so much to learn, so much to do, and—by the way—everyone's in the same boat! "I was afraid I'd hate sailing. But as soon as I took the helm, I loved it!" said 49-year-old Jane Candella. Taking the helm (driving the boat) is a blast. You're the one who decides when to change course, when to trim in the sails or ease them out. You're the one who feels the action and reaction of the boat first.

- **"I get seasick."** So do lots of sailors. But I doubt you'll get seasick in a sailing course. You're out in open boats, with the air in your face, and too busy to worry or think about feeling ill. Seasickness can sometimes be cured by steering, which forces you to concentrate on the sails and the horizon. On a cruise in Tahiti in long ocean swells, we shared 20-minute shifts on the helm and sang our hearts out. What was it about singing? Perhaps the fact that we were taking in more air, concentrating on remembering words, relaxing, and looking out to the horizon. Whatever it was, it worked! (See Chapter 6 for more remedies.)

- **"Sailing seems complicated."** Not at all—unless you choose to make it so. It's true there is a language to learn; but it's logical and full of words we use in everyday life. You can learn to sail in three 8-hour days or spread those 24 hours over a week or two. You never stop learning. But in a short time, you'll have the building blocks and the understanding for a lifetime of sailing fun.

- **"I'm a little person and not very strong."** So am I. Sailing skill is not dependent on strength. There are all kinds of boats and all kinds of equipment to put on boats that make sailing easy and fun for women of all shapes and size. I'll describe some of this gear—and ways to help make yourself stronger—in later chapters.

- **"I'm too old."** No one is too old. I know women who learned when they were in their seventies, including a 79-year-old who wanted to learn before she turned 80. There aren't many sports where women in their late thirties are still hotly competitive. But in sailing, there are—and these women are winning gold and silver medals and are decorated with national honors each year.

- **"I have a handicap."** I know women who sail with bad backs and other physical problems. I also know sailors who are blind and in wheelchairs. There are several groups that teach physically impaired students in sailboats that are specially adapted for this purpose (see the Resource Directory for information).

- **"I'm afraid in bad weather."** If you're lucky, you'll experience some strong winds during your lessons while your instructor is aboard. This is great preparation for sailing later on. Sailing is 90 percent bliss; it's that other 10 percent that hangs us up. In later chapters, I talk about safety gear and procedures, boat preparation, and how to handle rare but natural occurrences of sudden squalls and lightning storms.

- **"I don't want to be yelled at."** I call this crew abuse, and I don't like it either. Most people yell because they're inexperienced and uncertain. Some yell because they have abusive personalities. This phenomenon isn't exclusive to men.

The best precaution you can take is to learn to sail at an accredited school and be choosy about who you sail with afterwards. Sailing is a social sport. You can keep it that way when you have confidence in your own abilities.

- **"What about personal space, privacy, and creature comforts?"** Now you're getting into living aboard. Some of these issues are a mindset, but some are real issues and questions that would stop me if I didn't know how wonderful living aboard can be. How much personal gear can you bring aboard? As much as you need to feel at home. How do you get away and find privacy in such tiny living space? I specify at the beginning that I will need personal space and private time, and I designate an area that's all mine. When I'm there, I'm not there for anyone else but me. Can I bring my hair dryer, curling iron, do my nails? Yes and no. Cruising sailor Diana Jesse recently wrote a book for women that addresses these kinds of questions (see the Resource Directory).

- **"Can I really afford sailing?"** Sailing isn't expensive, unless you want it to be. You can sail all you want in many places and never own a boat. Plan on spending $25 to $35 an hour with a certified commercial sailing school, and around $85 for a 16-hour course at a community boating center. Some metropolitan areas (such as New York City and San Francisco) have sailing clubs with annual memberships that run less than $1,000 a season. Join one and you can sail all season without further commitments or costs, such as boat maintenance, dock or mooring fees, and insurance. When you become a boat owner, costs can range from a couple hundred dollars for a used boat—like a Laser or a Sunfish that you can put atop your car—to many thousands of dollars for a second home at sea or in a marina. The choice is yours.

- **"What are my chances to continue sailing if I don't buy a boat?"** There are many sailors who are not boatowners. Once you gain some skill, you will be valuable as a crewmember. Most boat owners need crew, and a good crew is like gold to an owner. You can meet other sailors in many ways: through friends, office mates, sailing magazines, sailing clubs, women's sailing associations, sailing schools, and even on the Internet. I've seen long-term friendships and marriages develop through the newfound common bond of sailing. Some of these relationships even stretch thousands of miles to opposite ends of the country.

- **"Is sailing safe?"** If you don't know how to handle a boat's lines and equipment, or you don't know where not to stand or sit, you could get in trouble. That's why I recommend going to a certified sailing school. Before I go off sailing on strange boats, I like to learn about the boat and the rest of the crew— even if we're only taking a short day sail. I want to know what condition the boat, rig, sails, and equipment are kept in; what safety gear is aboard and where it's stowed; what communication gear is onboard for contacting other boats, the Coast Guard, or someone on shore; what supplies the boat's medical kit contains. If we're going on a long-distance race or cruise, I want to know how the crew is prepared to handle a medical emergency.

You might slam into a tree while skiing, be thrown off a horse on a jump, or lose your footing in rock climbing. But hazards like these just don't exist in everyday recreational sailing. The chances of injury occurring on a sailboat are less than when crossing the street. Very little can go wrong on a simple sailboat designed for daysailing. Just enjoy!

STEP ABOARD

It's fairly easy to get aboard a sailboat at a dock, entering from the bow, stern, or side. If the dock is *fixed* (it does not float up and down with tidal movements) and the tide is very low, the step between the dock and the boat can be a big one—and the distance might be farther than you think. Don't take a flying leap! You might want to sit on the side of the dock and, holding onto a shroud (a wire that runs from the deck to the mast), lower yourself feet first aboard. If the boat is small and light, you'll feel some movement when you step aboard. Regardless of the boat's size, it's

Stepping aboard. Pass your gear to a helper aboard, then hold onto a lifeline or shroud and step quickly from dock (or launch) to boat.

prudent to step quickly and commit to the boat. Straddling, with one foot on the dock and one on the boat, is asking for trouble. Boats move, whether they're tied up or not, and you might find yourself in an ever-increasing split if you wait too long.

If you are boarding a boat on a mooring or at anchor, you'll probably be in a small outboard boat or in a launch (a powerboat used by yacht clubs and some sailing schools that is essentially your taxi between land and your boat). The launch comes alongside the sailboat and temporarily ties up (or someone will hold on) while you get aboard. The sailboat is typically pointing into the wind with little movement as you approach in the launch. But the wind, the current, or the wake

• •

"The mixture of learning, relaxing, and reaching a goal made learning to sail not only memorable, but self-satisfying. It has helped me not only on a boat, but in many other areas of my life."

—Andrea Louise Mason, age 38

• •

made by the dinghy or launch will make the sailboat move as you come alongside. Everyone loves to get into the act and help *fend off* (push the other boat away) or hang on as the two boats meet. Until you get used to this maneuver, let your instructors and the driver do the work of holding on or fending off—and always keep your hands away from the area between the two boats. If you are carrying any gear or personal items, pass these items over first, or ask someone to hand them to you after you're aboard. Then take hold of a shroud and step aboard quickly. Always commit to one boat or the other.

There's lots to do once aboard, but you'll soon get into the rhythm.

HOW DOES IT FEEL?

It's pretty amazing to be sitting comfortably on the high side of a sailboat as it leans with the force of the wind in its sails. At first you might feel unsteady. But you'll soon get into the rhythm. As you pull the sails in or let them out, you'll hear the boat accelerate as water rushes by. And you'll feel the boat *center* (reach a balance point) as changes are made.

When it's your turn to steer, the boat will react to your every move. At first, your movement might be too much and too far, or too little and not enough. After some time, you'll get the boat into a groove and feel it respond to your touch like a racehorse on its winning lap. As you look out to the horizon and feel the direction of the wind on your face, your grip will relax and your body will sway with the boat's motion. You're sailing!

Chapter 3

GETTING COMFORTABLE WITH SAILING

Part of the process of getting comfortable with sailing involves gaining knowledge about sailing and how boats and sails work. This is the get-acquainted chapter to give you enough information to step aboard and go sailing! The nomenclature may seem overwhelming at first, but it's all very logical and will quickly become a second language. But first, let's talk about what kind of boat you might start sailing on.

Sailboats come in all sizes and shapes—from lightweight dinghies to large, heavy cruising boats with lots of living space below.

A sailing dinghy can be under 10 feet or close to 20 feet in length. It can have room enough for just one or two people, in a space that feels at first like a tippy bathtub. Or it can have a big, somewhat daunting open area with trapezes and boards for crew to hang out on, with lots of sails and lots of jobs to keep them upright. Starting out on a high-performance dinghy, like the one described above, is like jumping into a Ferrari before learning to drive a Ford Taurus. Although popular in many kids' programs, I do not recommend small, low-performance dinghies for adults because they can capsize and don't provide enough room or variety.

> "**M**y first sailing experience, I didn't understand the concepts and principles of sailing. But I remember loving the feeling."
>
> —Jane Candella, age 49

Some racing sailors and kids start out in *board boats*. These boats have earned their name because you sit *on* the boat more than you sit *in* it. You are also apt to get wet more often than not, and you may need to be somewhat agile. True, a less forgiving dinghy or board boat is the best way to get a real *feel* for sailing. But unless your sights are set on that type of sailing for the long haul, make it easy on yourself!

A flotilla of board boats, called Bytes.

Community sailing schools, which are supported by donations and grants, offer courses throughout the country on boats ranging from 8 to 24 feet. Some are off-the-beach programs on shallow ponds and lakes, and some are in city harbors on rivers and estuaries. The smaller the training boat, the more likely your instructor will coach you from a *chase boat* (a small powerboat that can ride alongside your boat) instead of being onboard with you. You might have to pass a swim test and learn how to capsize the boat, turn it rightside up again, and get back on. Many of these programs focus on training for youth and the handicapped, as well as teaching adults. They encourage graduates to come back at very low rentals throughout the year.

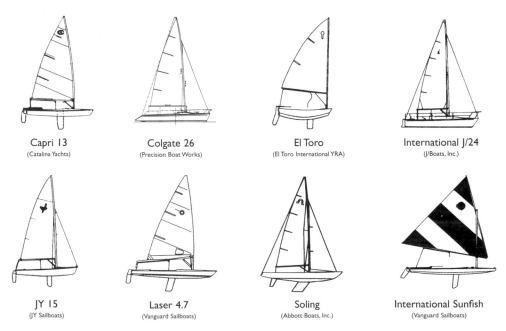

Capri 13
(Catalina Yachts)

Colgate 26
(Precision Boat Works)

El Toro
(El Toro International YRA)

International J/24
(J/Boats, Inc.)

JY 15
(JY Sailboats)

Laser 4.7
(Vanguard Sailboats)

Soling
(Abbott Boats, Inc.)

International Sunfish
(Vanguard Sailboats)

A sampling of some of the more popular brands of sailboats typically used by community and commercial sailing schools. (Courtesy boat manufacturers)

. . . .

"I LOVE sailing—the sense of freedom, peace, the exhilaration of being one with the wind and water."

—Stephanie Argyris, age 47

. . . .

I recommend starting out on a three- or four-person keelboat—a sailboat that's stable, responsive, allows mistakes, yet has enough options to promote a rapid learning curve. Of equal importance is your space onboard: you will have room to work, you won't feel confined, and your instructor can stay out of the way but be ready to jump in when necessary.

Since cruising is more popular than racing (many women who are new to the sport seem to prefer the tranquillity and comfort of cruising to competitive sailing), the transition to bulkier, sometimes larger cruising boats is far easier if you start on 20- to 30-foot keelboats.

After thirty-five years of teaching on 27-foot Olympic class Solings, we now use the Colgate 26, an award-winning cruiser designed specifically for teaching adults. Solings are still used by many other commercial schools, as are other keelboats such as the Sonar, J/22, and J/24. Stable and responsive, these boats are large enough to allow you to make mistakes without fear, yet small enough to give you a sense of the rhythm of sailing. They are also about the same size as most commercial rental fleets, and sophisticated enough to make the transition to larger boats easy.

Top: A typical cruising sailboat, the kind you might find on a Caribbean charter. **Bottom:** The Colgate 26: A stable and responsive keelboat, similar to the type found in many sailing programs. (The "26" in the name refers to the boat's length overall.)

Sailing student Jane Candella learned on one of our Solings, which is a very different boat, with lots of power and pizzazz compared to her heavier 32-foot cruising boat. "It was tough, but good for me," she remarked. "My boat is a piece of cake by comparison."

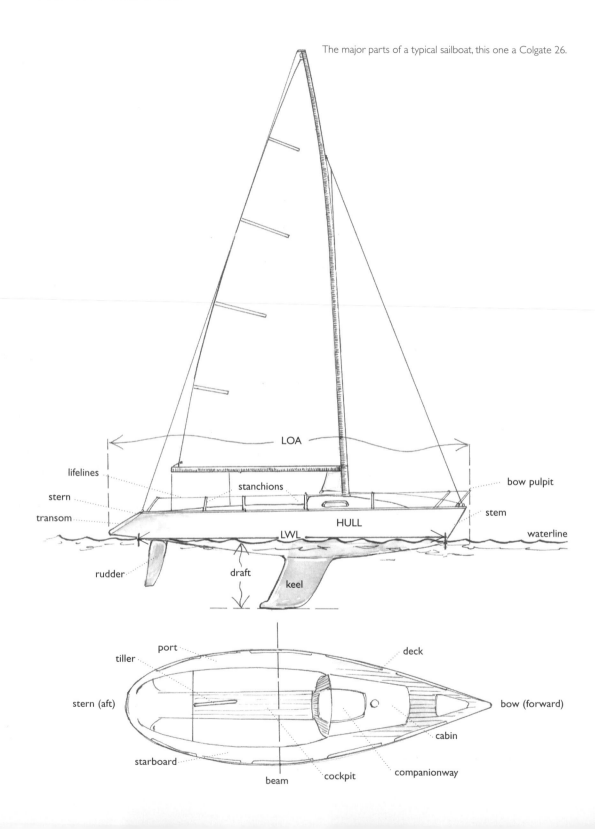

The major parts of a typical sailboat, this one a Colgate 26.

LOA

lifelines

stanchions

bow pulpit

stern

transom

HULL

stem

LWL

waterline

rudder

draft

keel

tiller

port

deck

stern (aft)

bow (forward)

cabin

starboard

beam

cockpit

companionway

SAILOR TALK

I used to race with crew from several different countries. We didn't share the same native tongue—and were it not for the common language of sailing, communication and teamwork would have been difficult!

Sailors around the world share the common language of sailing. I'll take you on a tour of a Colgate 26—the type of boat we teach on at Offshore Sailing School—to illustrate the basic terms that define the shape of a sailboat, the way a sailboat is measured and labeled, and the fittings and parts of the sails.

Step aboard and face the front (the pointy end). This is the *bow*, and as you move toward it you are *going forward*. Behind you, at the back end of the boat, is the *stern*. The term evolved from the Norwegian word *stjorn*, which means to steer. Generally speaking, sailboats are steered from the stern (or close to it). As you move toward the stern, you are *going aft*.

The platform you're standing on is the *deck*. The deck covers the *hull*, the floating receptacle in which everything else is placed. Long ago, boats were *hulled* (dug out) from logs. Later they were shaped with planks of wood. Today, most hulls are built from a fiberglass mold, although large sailboats are often made of aluminum.

Sailboats can have one hull or several, which is where the designations *monohull* (meaning one hull) and *multihull* (meaning several hulls) come from. The terms *catamaran* (for two hulls) and *trimaran* (for three hulls) are used to describe different types of multihulls. The catamaran, which means "tied wood," originated in the South Pacific. It was a raft of logs with an *outrigger*—a float positioned parallel to the raft and held away from the hulls by perpendicular supports. Its purpose is to provide stability and keep the boat from capsizing.

Walk back toward the stern to a molded area called the *cockpit*. Here you'll usually find seats and many of the boat's controls, including steering. As on an airplane, this is where you sit to maneuver the boat.

Now look forward to an opening under the deck. This is the *cabin*. It has places to lie down (called *berths*), and an area for a stove, portable sink, toilet, and electronics. When you go into the cabin, you pass through a *companionway* and you are *going below*. Conversely, when you come back *on deck* you say just that, or "I'm going *topsides*." Even though there are usually a few steps leading in and out of the cabin, the terms upstairs and downstairs are not used by seasoned sailors.

As you face the bow, the left side of the boat is the *port* side and the right side is the *starboard* side. It's easy to remember port because it has four letters, as does left. Starboard dates back to early ships, when the steering device (spelled *steor*) hung off the right side of the boat. When you sit on the left side of the boat, you're sitting on the port side. When another boat goes by on the right side, it's passing to starboard.

"I find that women learn terminology easily, because they have a will to understand."

—Kelley Jeffries, sailing instructor, age 36

HOW A SAILBOAT IS MEASURED

If you walk from the tip of the bow to the edge of the stern, and you add any part of the boat sticking out beyond the stern or the bow, that measurement is the *length overall*, or LOA—the distance in feet or meters along the boat's centerline from the forwardmost point of the boat to the rearmost point of the boat. LOA is important to know because it describes the boat's maximum length, which determines how much dock space you will use and pay for (calculated in dollars per foot) and how much distance (measured in *boat lengths*) there is between you and another boat or object.

The distance across the deck at the boat's widest point and perpendicular to its LOA is the *beam*.

Another measurement gives us the length of the boat at its waterline. The *waterline length*, or LWL, is measured on the horizontal plane where the hull floats on the water, from *stem to stern*. You might have used this expression when talking about an all-encompassing thought or project. The stem is the forward edge of the boat, which curves vertically down from the point where the bow meets the deck. On many modern sailboats, the stern at water level extends beyond the stern at deck level.

The depth of the boat, called *draft*, is the distance between the lowest part of the boat and the point where the boat floats on the water. It's important to know at all times if you're sailing in deep-enough water for the draft of your boat. The Colgate 26 measures (*draws*) 4 feet, 6 inches from the waterline to the bottom of the keel. If you try to sail it in an area with only 4 feet, 5 inches of water, you're going to touch bottom—with a variety of possible consequences. If you do touch bottom, it's called *going aground*—and most sailors eventually do. Like falling when you first learn to ski, you've just got to do it to learn how to get back up. I discuss how to avoid going aground, and how to get off if you do, in Chapter 5.

Other measurements you might run into, although they are not shown in the illustrations, are: *ballast*, which is the amount of weight in the keel; *displacement*, how much the boat weighs without sails; *sail area* (SA), the total area of the sails measured in square feet.

WHAT MAKES A SAILBOAT STABLE?

As you walk around the sailboat, you'll find it doesn't rock much. That's because it has a *keel* attached to the bottom of the hull. Remember the phrase, on an even keel? The keel is the stabilizing part of the boat and the deepest point of the boat in the water. Keels come in all sorts of shapes, weights, and lengths—but the most important thing to remember about a keel is it determines what depth of water you can sail in without touching the bottom.

Instead of a keel, some boats have a *centerboard*. A centerboard is a thin, blade-shaped piece of wood or fiberglass that is moved up and down in a slot near the center of the boat; it acts like a keel that can be moved. Small boats often have centerboards. When they're pulled all the way up, the boat can *plane* (skim) over the water on a thin air cushion in certain wind and wave

• •

"I started out with a lot of fear and hated heeling.
But I took the helm and saw what the boat could
do. Now, I find sailing exhilarating."

—Carol Ward, 45

• •

conditions. When the wind is pushing from behind, the boat remains fairly level with the horizon and doesn't need much weight below to keep the boat from heeling. If that weight can be raised, as it can on a centerboard boat, there's less drag through the water under the hull and the boat will go faster. But since overall stability and efficiency—and not necessarily speed—are more important when learning, and since centerboard boats can be tippy and harder to control, I prefer keelboats (a boat with a keel, as opposed to a centerboard) for teaching.

Why do sailboats have either a keel or centerboard? One reason is to keep the boat from slipping sideways when the wind pushes against the sails. More importantly, a keel or centerboard offsets the tipping or leaning over (*heeling*) created when a sailboat's sails are filled with wind. Think of a seesaw. Remember as a kid how you and a friend could both hang there evenly off the ground if you weighed about the same? On a sailboat, the force of the wind fills the sails and pushes them over, causing the keel (which is fairly heavy compared to the rest of the boat) to rise toward the surface. When properly designed, there is a balance point where the boat can move along nicely with the weight in the keel offsetting the weight of the wind in the sails.

Under the stern is the *rudder*, the blade at the back of the boat that steers the boat. In modern boats, the rudder is not normally visible when the boat is in the water. But in the photo at right, both the keel and rudder are visible in the Caribbean's crystal clear water.

TAKE CHARGE OF HEELING
• • • • • • • • • • • • • • • •

Heeling causes some of the greatest apprehension among new sailors. At first, when you heel you might tend to feel out of control as the boat you are on begins to lean over. But two things help cure that immediately: letting out one or more of the sails, and steering in a different direction. Carol Ward, a take-charge person, was apprehensive about sailing until she took the helm and found that she was able to control the boat's angle of heel.

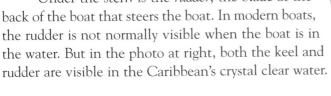

The **keel** and **rudder** of this sailboat are visible through the clear waters of the Caribbean.

Step toward the back of the cockpit and you'll find a *tiller*, which some sailors refer to as the *stick* (because that's what it looks like). The tiller is attached to the rudder, and if you push it back and forth a little, you'll feel a slight resistance. That resistance is the pressure created by the rudder pushing water aside as it's moved. Some sailboats are steered by a wheel. But most smaller boats (up to 30 feet) are steered by a tiller.

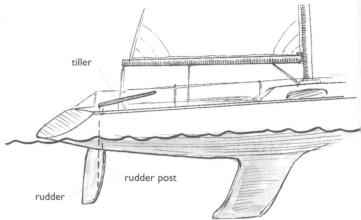

A typical tiller/rudder arrangement.

As a boat gets larger, a wheel makes steering easier. But the immediate reaction of the boat to your command is best felt on a boat with a tiller. It's sort of like learning to drive with a stick shift: you get the feel of how the gears work, and it's much more interesting and exciting.

You can steer a boat with sails alone. I will explain this in Chapter 5, and a good sailing school will have you practice this exercise. Knowing how to steer by sails alone is a valuable skill to have in the event that something happens to your boat's steering mechanism.

If you feel unsteady as you walk around the deck, hold onto the stainless steel guards and plastic-coated wire (called the *lifelines*) that run the length of both sides of the boat, about 3 feet above the deck. They're there for your safety. Most sailboats have stainless steel guards in the bow and stern, called the *bow pulpit* and *stern pulpit* (picture where a preacher gives a sermon). Flexible lifelines run through vertical posts, called *stanchions*. Some lifelines have gates on both sides and on the stern, so they can be opened for easy boarding.

HOW SAILS ARE HELD UP AND CONTROLLED

Now look up at the big pole aloft and the wires that connect it to the deck. These are the *mast* and *rigging*. A sailboat can have one mast or multiple masts. The term *rig* refers to how the mast (or masts) are arranged and held in place on a boat (see the box on different rigs, page 41).

Where the mast meets the deck is called the *mast step*. If the mast sits on the deck, it fits in a *shoe*. Or it extends through a *collar* on the deck to the interior below. The shoe keeps the mast from rubbing against deck surfaces where it sits. The mast can also extend through the reinforced collar on the deck and to a reinforced plate over the keel.

The mast is held upright by wire or rod rigging that attaches to the front, back, and two sides of the boat. Wire rigging is made of stainless steel wire, and rod rigging is simply a solid rod of stainless steel. These supports are the *standing rigging*, which is a pretty logical term since they just stand there and are seldom moved or adjusted while you sail.

Stand near the mast and look forward to the bow, then back to the stern. The wires you see are the *forestay* and *backstay* that keep the mast from falling back or forward. Both of these can be

SOME MODERN RIGS

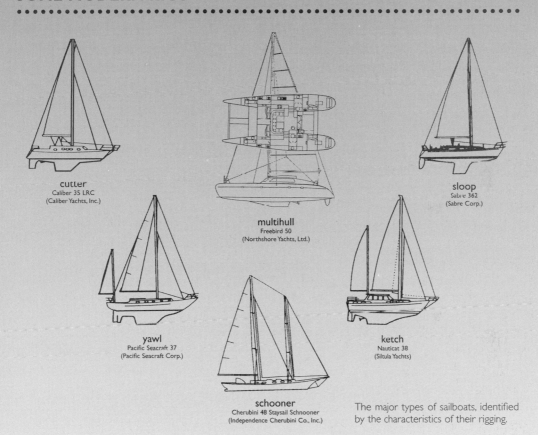

cutter
Caliber 35 LRC
(Caliber Yachts, Inc.)

multihull
Freebird 50
(Northshore Yachts, Ltd.)

sloop
Sabre 362
(Sabre Corp.)

yawl
Pacific Seacraft 37
(Pacific Seacraft Corp.)

ketch
Nauticat 38
(Siltula Yachts)

schooner
Cherubini 48 Staysail Schnooner
(Independence Cherubini Co., Inc.)

The major types of sailboats, identified by the characteristics of their rigging.

Sailboats with one mast are the most common. These can be *sloops* or *cutters*. The Colgate 26 is a sloop, and most new sailors learn on a sloop. The mast on a cutter is farther aft, and this creates a larger area forward for the *headsails* (the sails set forward of the mast). A sloop's mast is farther forward than a cutter's mast.

When a sailboat has a small mast in the back, called a mizzen mast, it's either a *ketch* or a *yawl*. A ketch or yawl is determined by the location of the *rudder post*, a post that vertically connects the tiller above deck to the rudder under the hull. If the mizzen mast is a fairly short mast with a small sail and located aft of the rudder post, the boat is a yawl. If the mizzen mast is

taller with a larger sail and is forward of the rudder post, the boat is a ketch. A schooner usually has a tall main mast near the middle of the boat and a shorter mast forward, but a schooner can also have multiple masts of the same height.

Why are there so many different rigs? Mostly, it's due to evolution and use. With new technology and design in both hull shape and sails, fewer masts that carry more efficient sails are generally better. Sloops and cutters are the most popular for this reason. Still, some long-distance cruising sailors like a split rig (a ketch or a yawl), which allows the boat to sail relatively comfortably in rough weather with just a mizzen sail and a jib (minus the bigger mainsail).

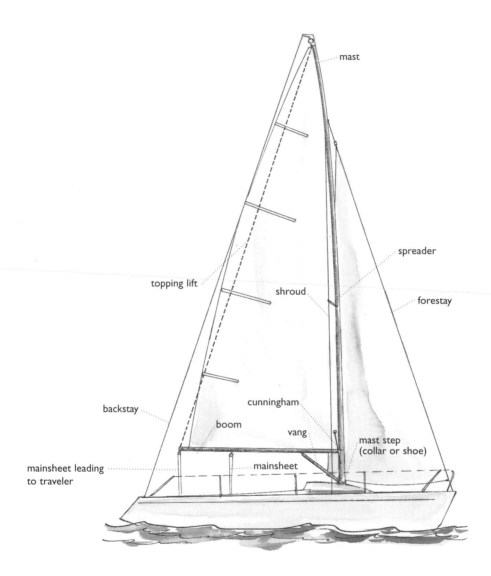

mast

spreader

topping lift

shroud

forestay

backstay

cunningham

boom

vang

mast step
(collar or shoe)

mainsheet leading
to traveler

mainsheet

A rigging diagram of a Colgate 26, showing the major parts of the **standing** and **running** rigging.

adjusted, and on sophisticated racing boats they are adjusted to change the shape of the sail for certain conditions. But when cruising or just sailing around, these two wires just *stay* where they were placed when the boat was rigged and set up for sailing.

Now look to the sides of the boat. The wires that reach down to the deck are the *shrouds*, which hold the mast upright from side to side. Look at the angles made between the mast and the forestay and the mast and the backstay. Now look at the angle made by the shrouds and the mast. You will notice that the angle between the shrouds and the mast is far more acute than the angles made by the fore and aft stays. *Spreaders* (vertical bars between the shrouds, placed at various levels) spread this angle and create better support. The tension in these shrouds is rarely changed, though they should be checked for proper tension from time to time.

Back in the cockpit, there's a tube or rectangular extrusion that extends horizontally from the mast called the *boom*. This is attached by a *gooseneck*, which allows the boom to swing from side to side and up and down. The boom helps support the sail, and there are a variety of fittings attached to it to both change the sail's shape and control the way the boat sails. The boom is an easy part of the boat to remember, since it can cause discomfort if it swings and your head happens to be in the way.

About a quarter of the way back from the mast and attached to the boom is the *boom vang*. This keeps the boom from skying (rising up). It also helps shape the sail in various conditions and wind directions. If the boom vang is a solid tube, it can also take over for the *topping lift*, which is a line that runs from the top of the mast to the end of the boom. Its purpose is to lift the end of the boom and keep it from falling to the deck.

About two-thirds of the way back and at the end of the boom you'll find rope that runs through pulleys. These are the *mainsheet* and *traveler*, part of the *running rigging* that moves (runs) sails in and out, up and down.

You'll find more rope and wire running vertically along the mast. These are the *halyards* you pull on or release to raise and lower the sails.

Ropes aboard a sailboat are almost always called *lines*. These lines run through channels and pulleys called *blocks* to reduce friction and provide more purchase (power) for easier and quicker maneuvering. Sailboat blocks are nothing like the playthings you used as a kid. Note how they're shaped, often oval and with rotating channeled rings that roll on ball bearings—a boon to those of us with less strength.

Lines used to adjust sails in and out are called *sheets*. One of the strangest word uses in sailing, this term apparently stems from the old English *sceatta* (pronounced *sheeta*), the point where a line is tied into a sail.

The *mainsheet* controls the largest sail (the *mainsail*) on the boat, and this is your first priority when it comes to keeping your boat at the correct angle to the wind. The mainsheet is also connected to the traveler, which does just that. It travels across the width of the boat where it is located and provides more help in maintaining control and keeping optimum shape in the sail for various conditions.

Jibsheets move the front and usually smaller sail (the *jib*) in and out. When you start to speak the language of sailing underway, you might be asked to *sheet in* a sail.

Now look around the cockpit and find the metal drums with holes in their flanged tops. These *winches* are placed strategically on the deck to help *trim* (pull in and let out) sails and shape them to capture the wind. Sheets are wound clockwise around a winch's drum, which is turned by a movable or fixed handle called a *winch handle* that fits into a socket in the top of the winch. The larger the winch, the easier it is to adjust lines and maintain control.

Sailing has come a long way in recent years, not only with larger winches but with mechanisms that make these winches like miniature robots that help us change the shape of sails with fewer hands. When you pull in a sail, the loose end of the line, called the *tail*, gets longer and

A self-tailing winch (*left*) and a winch with handle (*right*).

longer. The tail has to be kept taut or the person grinding the winch handle will just spin her wheels. You can crank with one hand and pull the tail with the other, but this is not the most efficient arrangement; tailing is generally done with a helper. An arrangement that is increasingly popular, and often more efficient, is to have winches that are *self-tailing*. A self-tailing winch has a holding device (a *cleat*) in the top that takes the place of another person.

HOW TO TALK ABOUT SAILS

Sails are a sailboat's engine. Their shape, material, construction, and how they're *set* (positioned to the wind) determine how fast and efficiently a sailboat will move. Materials and construction can be state of the art, with space-age names and technology. Though exotic sails made from materials like Kevlar and Mylar are used on many racing boats, Nylon and Dacron sails are found on boats like the Colgate 26. These sails are manipulated by the same efficient blocks, pulleys, and winches found on hot racing boats, which make it easy to adjust sails and do ordinary maneuvers without brute strength. All you need are the brains and desire, which you have, and the know-how, which you'll soon get!

On a sloop like the Colgate 26, the mainsail and jib both have a triangle shape. Imagine that you're going out for the first time, and both sails are already rigged and ready for sailing. Face forward and look at the mainsail first. The front of that sail, the forward edge, is called the *luff*. It's held in the channel on the aft side of the mast by rope sewn into the edge of the cloth. This is called the *boltrope*. Some older boats have plastic toggles sewn along the luff instead. These toggles also run up the groove (or track) in the mast, but they are not as efficient. (You'll learn more about the efficiency of sail shape in Chapter 7.)

Look along the bottom of the sail, called the *foot*. Note that a boltrope there also runs through a groove in the boom. The *tack* is where the luff and the foot meet at the forward, lower

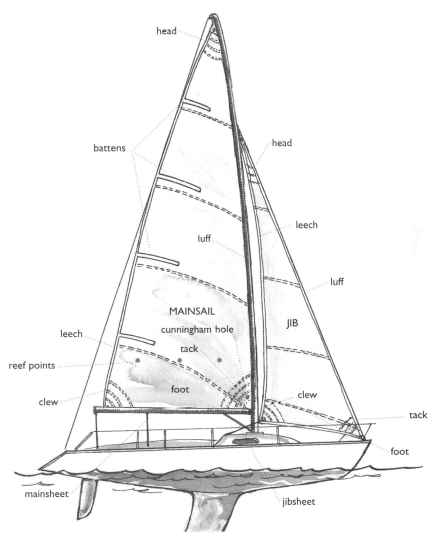

The major parts of a **mainsail** and **jib**.

corner of the sail. In the old days, this corner was actually tacked to the mast with hammer and nail. Marked by the sailmaker's label and a hole reinforced with a metal ring called a *grommet*, the tack is now kept firmly in place by a removable hook or *shackle* (a metal clasp used as a link in many places on a boat, such as when connecting a halyard to the top of a sail).

Follow the back edge of the sail from the top of the mainsail to the foot at the end of the boom. This is the *leech*. Since this is the hardest place for a sail to hold its shape, there are pockets sewn horizontally at various intervals across the sail. *Battens*—which are thin, flexible sticks of wood or plastic—fit into these pockets to help shape the sail, like bones in an old-fashioned girdle.

The corner where the leech and foot come together is called the *clew*. The clew also has a reinforced hole for a hook or shackle, which is attached to the *outhaul*, a line that adjusts the sail in or out along the boom and makes it flatter or baggier along the foot.

● ●

"I remember my first time on the water. It was relaxing, exhilarating. My thoughts about the rest of life seemed to disappear."

—Denise Theri, age 49

● ●

Look up the mainsail to the top where the luff and the leech meet. This is the *head*. Note that it's reinforced with additional layers of cloth, or with a stiffener, to take the strain it endures when hauled up and kept in place. There's a shackle in the grommet in the head, which is attached to the *main halyard*. This is a long length of wire and rope that runs down the mast to a cleat that holds it in place. On smaller boats, the halyard is often all rope. Although you can't see it at the top of the mast, the halyard runs over a *sheave* (a grooved wheel or pulley) that helps alleviate friction and wear and tear as the sail is pulled up and down.

The mainsail still has more adjustments for comfort and ease of handling. Note the three horizontal levels of holes running from the leech to the luff. These are *reef points*, and they allow you to make the sail smaller (which is known as *shortening sail*) when the wind is too strong for the boat's maximum sail area. When you shorten sail, you depower the boat—which is like taking your foot off the accelerator in a car.

A *leech line* that runs vertically along the leech, in a channel sewn into the cloth, can be tightened or loosened to change the shape of the back edge of the mainsail. A *cunningham* (named after the man who invented it) at the lower end of the luff changes the shape of the forward edge of the mainsail.

Now look at the sail in the front of the boat. This is the jib on a Colgate 26. When the bottom, aft corner of the jib extends aft of the mast, the jib is called a *genoa*, or "genny" for short. A jib and a genoa are both headsails. Some larger boats, particularly racers, carry a variety of headsails of various sizes for different wind strengths and conditions.

The three edges and the corners of a headsail have the same names as the mainsail: The tack is where the luff (the front edge) meets the foot (the bottom edge); the clew is where the leech (the back edge) meets the back part of the foot; the head is where the luff meets the leech. The sailmaker's label is at the tack, just as it is on the mainsail, and both ends of the foot have a reinforced hole.

On some boats, the sail is fastened at the tack to an adjustable *downhaul*. A shackle or hook comes up through the deck in the bow, and the downhaul tightens or eases the luff of the sail.

The jib halyard is attached to the head of the jib, and the halyard raises the sail to the top of the mast along the forestay. Sometimes, a shorter jib has a wire *pennant* (a length of wire with a hole or shackle at the top) that is attached to the head to make up the distance to the top of the mast.

The jib on the Colgate 26 rolls up around the forestay. When you are finished sailing, or if it's too windy to use your jib, the sail is wrapped all the way around the forestay. The jib can also be wrapped partway around the forestay, leaving a smaller triangle of sail to better balance your boat in high winds. This arrangement is called *roller-furling*, and the system is typically found on many cruising boats. On the Colgate 26, the wire in the luff of the jib is the boat's forestay.

Look at the drum just below the tack of the jib and follow the *reefing line* from that drum to the block on the port side of the cockpit. To open up the sail (pull it out), you pull on a jibsheet and release the reefing line. As the sail is released, the jib opens and the reefing line winds around the drum. To roll the sail in, you simultaneously pull the reefing line and ease the jibsheets. All these maneuvers are done from the cockpit.

Look at the clew (the bottom corner of the jib) where the foot and the leech meet. Note that two lines are tied into a reinforced hole. One leads to the right side of the cockpit, and one leads to the left side. These are the jibsheets

A **roller-furling drum** for a jib.

that wind around the winches on either side of the cockpit. The big difference between the mainsail and jib, during certain maneuvers, is that the mainsail can move from one side of the boat to the other by sliding along the traveler, and you don't have to handle the lines. The jib, however, must be adjusted by the crew who release the tension in the jibsheet on one side and pull in the sheet on the other side. There is an exception. Some boats have a jib track in front of the mast that allows the jib to slide from one side to the other, just like the main.

BASIC SAILBOAT MOVES

The angle and pressure of the wind on the sails make a sailboat move. To understand how and why this happens, you first need to understand the basic maneuvers you use to change the direction of a sailboat: *tack, jibe, fall off,* and *head up.*

A sailboat can't sail directly into the wind, but it can sail at a fairly close angle to the wind. If the direction you want to go in is directly into the wind (called *dead upwind*), then you'll have to tack: move the boat from one side of the wind to the other. When you tack upwind you sail a zig-zag path, which is called a *beat* (see illus-

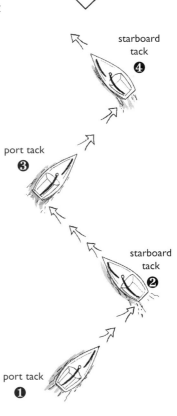

WIND

starboard tack ❹

port tack ❸

starboard tack ❷

port tack ❶

Above: Sailing upwind on a **beat**—a series of 90-degree zig-zags from port tack to starboard tack and back. The boat is **close-hauled**—sailing as close to the wind as possible. **Left:** The boat on the left is on a port tack; the boat on the right is on a starboard tack. Both boats are close-hauled.

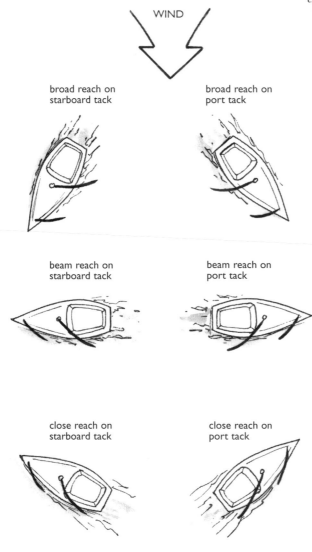

WIND

broad reach on
starboard tack

broad reach on
port tack

beam reach on
starboard tack

beam reach on
port tack

close reach on
starboard tack

close reach on
port tack

Top: Starboard and port tack on a reach.

tration). When executed smoothly, tacking back and forth feels like a series of rhythmic moves. The tighter you keep the angle to the wind, while still maintaining your speed, the faster you'll get to your destination.

When the sails are in as tight as they can be and the boat is moving forward, the boat is *close-hauled*. Think of this as the wind pulling (*hauling*) the boat forward with the sails as close to the center of the boat as possible.

When the mainsail and jib are at any angle over the right (starboard) side of the boat, the boat is on a *port tack*. When the sails are over the left (port) side of the boat, the boat is on a *starboard tack*.

You are on a *reach* when the wind is coming from a direction perpendicular to the boat, or just ahead or behind that perpendicular line. Depending on that angle of the wind to the boat, you will be on a *broad reach*, a *beam reach*, or a *close reach*.

There's nothing tricky about these descriptions. A close reach starts when the sails are no longer as close to the centerline as possible and the wind is between the bow and the middle (beam) of the boat. When the wind is perpendicular to the hull, you are on a beam reach. As the wind begins to hit the boat in the area between perpendicular and the stern of the boat, you are on a broad reach.

If the wind direction is flowing toward the boat from directly behind you, you're sailing *dead downwind* and the mainsail will be straight out over the starboard side of the boat (or straight out over the port side). When you're sailing with the wind from behind, and you turn the boat so the sails switch from one side of the boat to the other, you are *jibing*.

When you are sailing dead downwind, the main is so far out that it can hide, or *blanket*, the jib from the wind. This causes the jib to flop around. When this happens, you might be able to pull the jib over to catch the wind on the opposite side of the boat. Looking like the wings of a bird, this point of sail is called sailing *wing and wing*.

When you change the direction of the boat, but you don't move the sail from one side to the other, you are either *falling off* (falling away from the wind) or *heading up* (heading up toward the wind). You'll learn more about heading up and falling off in the following section.

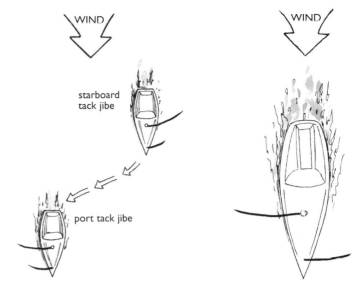

Left: Jibing from starboard to port. **Right:** sailing wing and wing on port tack (main is out over starboard side).

TAKING A SAILBOAT THROUGH ITS PACES

Let's go back to your close-hauled course. As you turn the boat away from the wind, while staying on the same tack, you're *falling off* (some say *bearing away*). As you fall off, ease both sails out

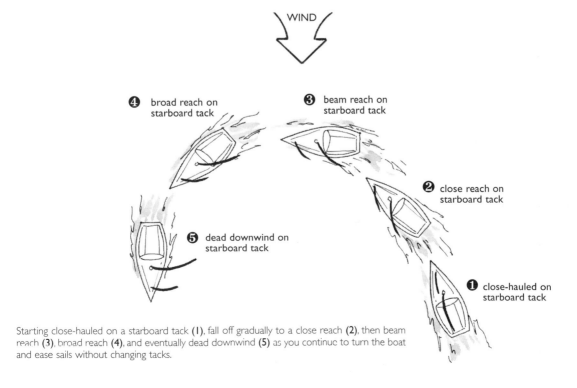

Starting close-hauled on a starboard tack (1), fall off gradually to a close reach (2), then beam reach (3), broad reach (4), and eventually dead downwind (5) as you continue to turn the boat and ease sails without changing tacks.

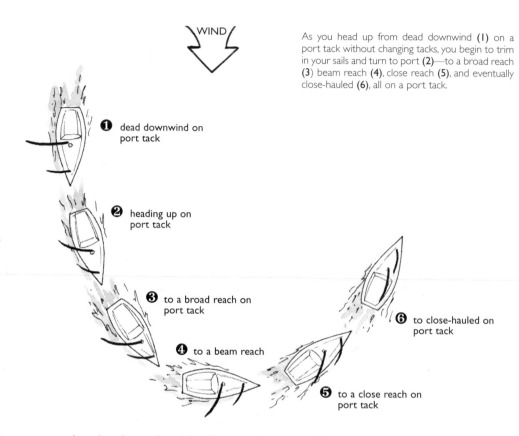

WIND

As you head up from dead downwind (1) on a port tack without changing tacks, you begin to trim in your sails and turn to port (2)—to a broad reach (3) beam reach (4), close reach (5), and eventually close-hauled (6), all on a port tack.

❶ dead downwind on port tack

❷ heading up on port tack

❸ to a broad reach on port tack

❹ to a beam reach

❺ to a close reach on port tack

❻ to close-hauled on port tack

to maintain your speed and sail comfortably. You can keep on falling off until you are headed 180 degrees, or directly opposite, from your original direction. If you continue to move the boat in the same direction, you come to a point where you're dead downwind.

The boat in the bottom illustration on page 49 is shown falling off from a close-hauled, starboard-tack course to a dead downwind, starboard-tack course. If this boat kept falling off past dead downwind, the wind would start to hit the sails from an angle that would flip them to the other side of the boat, which is called jibing.

If you want to go back to your original close-hauled course, or back upwind toward the direction the wind is blowing from, you turn the boat toward the wind and *head up*. The boat in the illustration above is shown heading up from a dead downwind, port-tack course to a close-hauled, port-tack course. The more you head up, the more you have to pull in your sails to maintain forward motion until you're finally heading directly into the wind. At this point, you have to tack.

Suppose you start close-hauled, fall off to a reach, continue moving away from the wind, and end up dead downwind. You want to keep turning in the same direction, so you jibe and start heading up on the opposite tack to a reach, and eventually to a close-hauled course again. You have just sailed in a circle and taken your boat through all the *points of sail* (see right).

To maintain speed through the water you had to constantly *trim* (pull in) or *ease* (let out) your sails. You ease out as you fall off and pull in as you head up. When the wind is ahead of you,

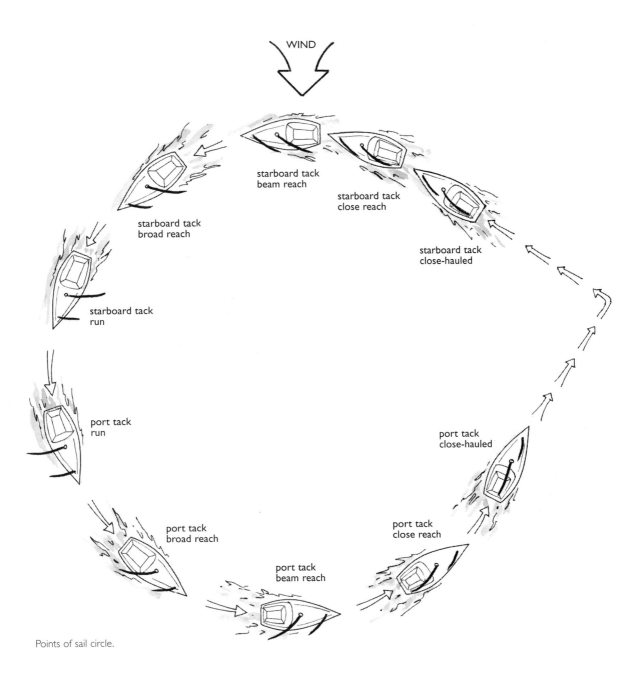

Points of sail circle.

When the boat is headed dead into the wind, both sails are **luffing**—streaming aft like a flag.

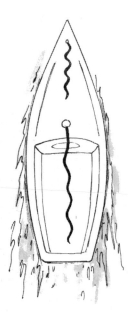

at the point where your sails are no longer filled (i.e., they are hanging limp or fluttering), your sails are *luffing*.

Sails will also start to luff if they're eased out too far on a reach or downwind course. They can also luff if the wind direction shifts and starts to come from ahead, or if you change the direction you are steering in relation to the wind without adjusting your sails. Whatever the reason, the results are generally the same: loss of speed and control. The sails start to shake because the wind no longer fills them, and the main boom will start to swing back and forth across the boat unless you tighten it up. If you're close-hauled or on a reach, the boat heels less and then straightens up. In all cases, the boat slows down and eventually stops because your engine, the sails, are stalled. Your boat can move backward or swing off in one direction or another. Just like driving a car: no gas, no forward momentum; no wind in your sails, no forward momentum. The better your sails are trimmed for the direction and strength of the wind, the faster your boat will go.

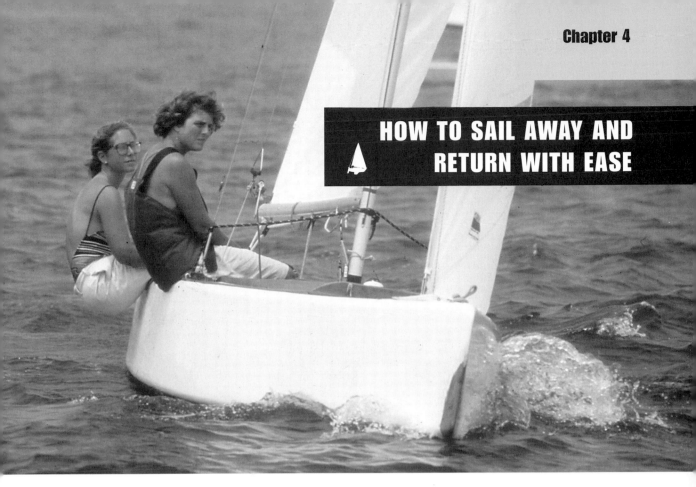

Chapter 4

HOW TO SAIL AWAY AND RETURN WITH EASE

You're onboard, it's a sunny day with a gentle breeze, and it's time to go sailing. Your instructor explains how you're going to leave the dock and gives each of you a job. Soon you're underway. You're on the helm, steering out of the marina, and the others are busy trimming sails with gentle directions from your instructor. During the day, you practice what she went over in class that morning. It's a lot, and you wonder, "How will I remember all this?" But with each maneuver, you understand more—and you know how Deborah Loeff felt after her first day at sailing school when she said, "When can I do this again?"

> "**R**esponding to the feel of the boat was so easy to learn. I just relaxed and let it move with me."
>
> —Marion Kaminitz, age 43

RIG AND HOIST THE SAILS

Most larger sailboats are equipped with roller-furling jibs and mainsails that are left *flaked* (folded) on the boom. On smaller boats, sails are usually taken off the boat and stored in bags. Let's assume the sails are not in place on your first day out.

Slide the mainsail's foot into the groove in the boom until it stretches from one end to the other. Fasten the tack to the gooseneck, where the mast and boom meet. Then, attach the clew to the shackle at the outboard end.

Before you raise the sail, place the battens into the pockets along the leech. Make sure each batten is pushed all the way into its pocket and secured under the flap at the outboard end so the batten can't fly out as you sail. Battens are usually graduated in size; be sure to put them in their correct pockets.

Before you attach the main halyard, make sure the halyard is running free and not twisted with any lines or other halyards. Check the luff to make sure the sail is not twisted. Start at the tack and run your hands down that edge. When you get to the head, place the head in the lower part of the groove on the mast and attach the halyard. Check a few more things before hoisting the sail: The mainsheet, boom vang, and reefing lines should be loose. Make sure the boat is pointed into the wind before hoisting the sail.

While you're working on the mainsail, someone else can work on the jib. First, fasten the tack of the sail (at the forward end of the foot) to a shackle attached to the bottom of the forestay. Then clip (or *hank*) the jib on. Start at the bottom of the sail, not the top. Why start at the bottom? If you start at the top, you'll have to hold up the cloth above while you struggle to hook the hanks on underneath.

Before you raise the jib, run your hands along the foot to make sure it's straight. This ensures the sail is not twisted. Make sure the jibsheets are tied into the clew and lead the sheets back through the appropriate blocks and winches on either side of the cockpit.

Top: Place the head of the sail in the lower part of the groove on the mast and attach the halyard. **Above:** When hanking on the jib, start at the bottom of the sail, not the top.

On many boats, jibs and genoas slide up grooved forestays. If this is the case, first put the head into the *pre-feeder*, a channel that funnels the sail into the groove, then attach the halyard. Before you attach the halyard, look up to make sure it's free and outside the shrouds. Before the sail is completely hoisted, attach the tack to the base of the forestay.

When you're ready to get underway, raise the mainsail first. While you're hoisting, look up to make sure the halyard or leech isn't caught around a shroud, and make sure the sail isn't twisted. If you encounter resistance on the way up, pull down on the luff to free any pinched material. If the resistance persists, stop and assess what's wrong before you pull harder and break something.

If there's a halyard winch, haul the halyard by hand until you can't pull anymore. Then put

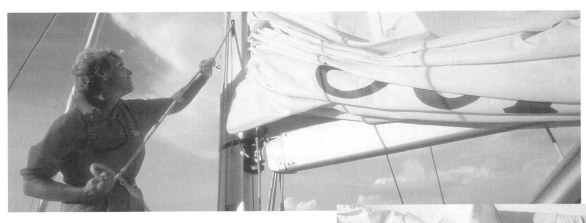

Above: To hoist the mainsail, haul down on the halyard coming out of the mast. **Right:** The winch in the cockpit is used to continue raising the mainsail when there's too much tension to do it by hand.

three clockwise turns around the winch and continue pulling the main up until the top of the head reaches a black band at the top of the mast. If there is no black band, pull the sail up until the luff looks nice and tight. Then cleat the halyard.

While the sail is luffing, tighten up the outhaul and downhaul (if there is one), and take up the slack in the reefing lines. If you have a topping lift holding the boom up, loosen it to free the leech of the sail.

Before getting underway, coil the excess halyard and tidy up the mainsheet so it can run freely. Make sure the mainsheet has a stop knot in its end (see instructions for making a stop knot, page 108). The mainsail should still be luffing, so keep clear of the swinging boom as you work.

What would happen if you tightened up the mainsheet to keep the boom from swinging? Remember, you're still attached to a mooring, anchor, or dock. If you tightened the mainsheet, you'd start sailing around your mooring or pulling against your docklines, which would make it difficult to untie and sail off.

When the mainsail is up and still luffing, raise the jib. Pull the sail up while someone makes sure the jib doesn't bind in the groove, and look up to make sure the sail isn't twisted and the halyard isn't caught. Make sure the jib reaches the top of the forestay and the luff is tight. The halyard usually runs down the mast on the port side (with the main halyard on starboard). Cleat the halyard and tighten up on the downhaul (if you have one). The jibsheets will probably be flailing around and could get twisted. It's okay to bring them back loosely to the winches, with one turn around each winch. Make sure a stop knot is tied into the free ends of the jibsheets. Sails lose some of their life if you allow them to flail too often in the wind—and they also make an unsettling racket.

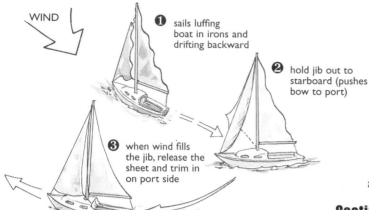

WIND

❶ sails luffing boat in irons and drifting backward

❷ hold jib out to starboard (pushes bow to port)

❸ when wind fills the jib, release the sheet and trim in on port side

Backing the jib to get underway.

As soon as you're ready, cast off and set sail!

GETTING UNDERWAY

Your boat might be tied to a mooring or anchored, in which case you'll get to it by launch or rowboat. Or it might be waiting for you at a dock, which makes it easy to step aboard but a little harder to get underway.

Casting off from a mooring or anchor

If your boat is tied to a mooring, all you do when you leave is release the mooring line. If you're anchored, the process takes more time because the anchor comes with you. Don't laugh. I've actually seen inexperienced sailors untie the anchor line on the bow and watch it sink. This is costly and very inconvenient.

At a mooring or at anchor, the boat swings and lines up with the wind, unless the current is stronger and from a different direction than the wind. Before you release the boat, raise the mainsail. Leave the mainsheet loose enough so the sail can swing and line up with the wind like a wind vane. In light air you can raise your jib too. In heavy air, wait to raise your jib; you'll avoid unnecessary flogging of the sail and tangled jibsheets.

If you have a roller-furled jib, you can pull it out after the anchor is up. If you need to rig your jib, do this first, attach the halyard, and make sure the sheets are led back to the winches. Then, drop the mooring or bring up the anchor, tighten the mainsheet to a close-hauled course, and you should be underway. If it's a windy day, hoist your jib now.

If you have trouble getting forward momentum or the boat is drifting backward because of strong wind or current, you might have to *back* the jib to get going. To do this, hold the jib out to windward (the direction the wind is coming from) as far as you can. As the sail fills, you'll feel the bow swing to leeward (away from the wind). To start sailing ahead, drop the sheet you're holding out to windward and simultaneously pull the sheet on the leeward side in quickly. Make sure you don't drift backward or sideways into other moored or anchored boats.

If you're in a tight anchorage or mooring field, stay tied to the mooring until your sails fill, then immediately drop the mooring line. If you're anchored, this is trickier. You can, however, get momentum as you pull up on the anchor and create forward motion. As the anchor is freed from the ground (you'll feel it), start trimming the sails while the rest of the anchor line is hauled aboard.

Casting off from a dock

When you cast off from a dock, many variables come into play—wind direction and strength, current, proximity to other boats—but the principles are the same. To hoist the sails, you want the bow pointed into the wind. Sometimes, this means you have to turn the boat around with lines or paddle to a better position.

Let's say the boat is docked with its bow facing the dock (called *bow in*) and the wind is coming from dead ahead. A line from your bow leads to a cleat on the dock, and a stern line is tied to a piling or mooring buoy behind you, or to a cleat on the outboard end of a dock alongside. You can easily raise your mainsail and drift back out of the slip with a lot of help from the wind and a little help from your crew. They can walk the boat back while making sure the sheets are loose and sails are luffing. As soon as your bow clears any boats or docks alongside, trim in the main, hoist the jib, and trim both sails, using the techniques you learned for getting away from a mooring.

If the wind is on your stern or coming from the side, ideally you should turn the boat to face into the wind before hoisting any sails by retying it in the *slip* (or dock space) while you prepare. You might have to paddle the boat to an unobstructed area where you can hoist your sails comfortably.

Whenever you are around other boats and obstacles, such as docks and sea walls, make sure you have *fenders* (soft, air-filled, sausage-shaped objects used to absorb impact). Fenders are usually tied onto the side of the hull while you are at dockside or near other obstacles; then they are stored out of the way. It's common to forget the fenders are hanging over the side in the heat of getting underway. Don't forget to take them off and stow them in a locker on deck or below as soon as

things calm down. When you are in proximity to obstacles, such as when you are leaving or returning to a crowded marina, one crew should hold a loose fender and be ready to dangle it over the side between your boat and an obstacle, such as a piling or another boat.

Most boats without engines are left on moorings, sailed off a beach, or berthed at a dock where the prevailing wind helps you leave gracefully. Most marinas are fairly protected from heavy winds, allowing boats to get underway with a minimum of problems. And most sailboats berthed in marinas have engines for leaving or returning to docks. An engine can keep your boat headed into the wind while you hoist your sails.

Leaving a dock under sail when the wind is on your bow.

When returning to the dock, make sure your fenders are ready.

SAILING AT LAST

You're on the helm, and it feels great. You are sitting in the back of the cockpit, another classmate sits in the middle of the cockpit to handle the mainsheet, and the others sit in the forward part of the cockpit to handle the jibsheets.

On a beat or reach, with a nice breeze heeling the boat, everyone sits on the high, windward side until it's time for a maneuver. Not only is this more comfortable, but the crew weight helps balance the boat by counteracting heeling.

In very light winds, the boat sails better if you force it to heel just enough to put some shape in the sails and fill them with what little wind you have. In this case, the crew sits on the low, leeward side of the boat. If you're steering and you can't see the jib or other boats from the low side, reposition yourself so you can see.

In a moderate to heavy breeze, steer from the high side where you can see the jib and keep the boat *in the groove*—that exhilarating feeling when the boat is trucking along smoothly and the helm feels perfectly balanced!

Every now and then, a crewmember should pop down to the low side of the boat and look under the jib to make sure the path ahead is clear. In light air, with everyone on the low side, you all might be able to see well. Still, one person should always be designated as a lookout and feed information to you as you steer. When you do make course changes to tack, jibe, or steer clear of an obstacle, always tell your crew what you plan to do so they are prepared for the maneuver.

If you're sailing dead downwind without too much wind or sea, the boat will be relatively flat and the crew can move around, ever mindful of the boom in case of an inadvertent jibe. This is when I like to go below to use the toilet, take off a layer, or get some water.

Top: Cockpit crew positions: helmsperson at the tiller, mainsheet handler in the middle, and the most forward seat reserved for the jibsheet tender. **Middle:** Everyone sits on the high side of the boat in heavy air. **Bottom:** In light air the boat moves nicely with the crew sitting on the low side.

Steering . . . a woman's touch

"Women excel at steering. We have a better sense of rhythm or coordination—perhaps because of all those years dancing backwards," says 75-year old instructor Betty Pearce. World-class racer Betsy Alison, 37, probably hasn't spent much time dancing backwards, but she believes women have a natural aptitude for steering because they concentrate better over long periods.

Steering relies a lot on feel, which is why it helps to have a little *helm*—a slight tug on the tiller—to keep the boat in the groove. If a tiller or wheel feels wishy-washy, you're more apt to move it around too much, which is a common problem for beginners. Slight, subtle movements are best.

Steering a boat with a wheel is a lot like driving a car. When you want to move from right to left, turn the wheel counter-clockwise and the bow will swing to the left while the stern swings to the right.

It's more likely, however, that you'll learn on a boat with a tiller, which is different from wheel steering. The basic rule for steering with a tiller is: Always push it *away* from the direction you want to go.

A sailboat changes direction as the rudder's angle to the flow of water changes. If the boat is going straight downwind and you want to turn to the left (port), move the tiller to the right (starboard). Water pushes against the rudder on its left side, the stern moves to the right, pivoting the bow to the left.

If the sails are trimmed correctly, you should be able to hold the tiller lightly, counteracting a slight tug or *weather helm*. Only on a run (dead downwind) do you want a *neutral helm* (no pull to one side or the other). When the sails are working well and the rudder is in line with the keel (or just slightly offset), you're not fighting the tiller; you're holding it in place with a little resistance.

If you find the tiller pulling away from you too much, the boat is not balanced and

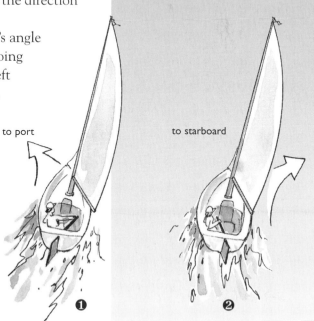

to port   to starboard

❶   ❷

To get comfortable steering with a tiller, with the boat on a port tack, push the tiller to right to turn the boat to port (1)—the stern goes right and bow goes left. To turn the boat to starboard (2) pull the tiller towards you—the stern goes left and bow goes right.

the rudder might be at too much of an angle in relation to the flow of the water. Think of a car that needs its wheels aligned: you're constantly oversteering to one side or the other, and when you take your hand off the wheel, the car veers to one side.

Time your steering maneuvers to the rhythm of the waves and your crew. Here are some useful hints:

- In a tack, watch the crew as they work on trimming the jib on the new side and move the bow under the sail as it comes across.

- If you see a wave coming from behind when you're off the wind, to maximize speed and increase control, steer up to wait for it and then down as it picks up your stern.

- Always try to warn your crew when you anticipate making changes.

- Use slight or subtle moves on the helm, and your crew won't have to do something special to offset a drastic change.

HOMEWARD BOUND

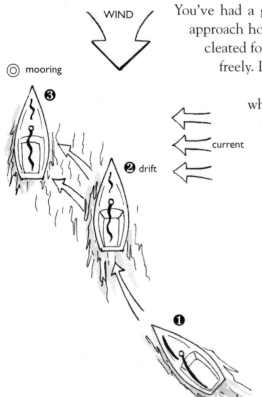

You've had a great day sailing and now it's time to head home. As you approach home port, prepare to get your sails down. Keep your halyards cleated for now, but make sure the halyards are coiled so they will run freely. Loosen the outhauls and downhauls.

Many larger sailboats have outboard or inboard engines, which make docking and anchoring quite easy. However, you can't always depend on an engine, but you can depend on your sails. It's important to learn how to get home under sail alone.

Back to the mooring

To pick up a mooring, sail toward it on a close reach or close-hauled. Turn into the wind when you are directly downwind of the mooring. You will drift to the buoy as your sails luff and the wind slows your boat down. Get used to the momentum of your boat and the distance it takes to stop under various wind conditions. You might have to allow for current and aim for the up-current side

To pick up a mooring under sail, with the current pushing you at right angles to the wind: sail close-hauled toward the mooring (1); when you are about a boat length away turn into the wind and let the sails luff (2); the current will then push you into the mooring (3).

of the buoy, so you can drift down into the buoy as you slow down. If the wind is strong, lower the mainsail and sail up to the mooring under jib alone. As you tie up, allow your sails to luff. Everything should be loose: mainsheet, boom vang, jibsheets.

Some mooring buoys have a tall pennant that you can easily reach from the deck. If there isn't one, use a *boat hook* (an extendable pole with a hook on the end) or reach down from the deck at the bow and scoop the buoy up out of the water. Always pick up a mooring buoy from the bow, not from the side or stern of your boat. Bring any attached mooring lines aboard *under* any lifelines. The mooring buoy stays in the water. If there is a pennant, it comes onboard. Tie the line quickly to your bow before the boat starts to drift back and puts tension on the mooring line. Then lay the pennant on deck. As soon as the boat is secure, lower your sails.

Anchoring under sail

First, get your anchor ready on the bow of the boat, with the anchor line (the *rode*) attached and led under all lines, lifelines, and the bow pulpit. Secure the free end of the rode to a cleat or an eye in the bow. As you sail around, pick the spot you want to anchor, and approach it the same way you approached your mooring.

Anchoring should be a controlled, easy maneuver. When

* *

"It was my first turn to take the helm and anchor. As we approached the harbor my fingers froze on the helm. All I could see was a sea of masts! . . . I checked the chart and picked a neat little spot, asked my crew to stand by while I slowly maneuvered between two boats, and gave the command to drop the anchor as soon as the boat came to a stop. It was great! We ended up in perfect position, with plenty of room to swing. High fives for us all!"

—Marcia Thompkins, age 59

* *

CHOOSING AN ANCHORAGE
• • • • • • • • • • • • • • • • • • •

Choosing a spot to anchor in depends on how crowded the anchorage is, the depth of the water, the tide, and the prevailing wind direction. If no other boats are in the area, your main concerns are: How close will my boat be to shore once I anchor? Are there any obstructions the boat might hit when it swings? If the anchorage is crowded, you might have to settle for a spot pretty far out to avoid swinging into boats already there. Generally speaking, the farther you are away from shore, the windier and choppier it can be (assuming you've chosen a harbor that's in the lee, or protected from the wind).

the boat comes to a complete stop, lower the anchor off the bow. As it touches the bottom, you'll feel the line in your hand go *soft*, with no pressure or weight on it. Keep easing more anchor line out. By now your boat should be drifting backwards.

How much *scope* is enough? Scope is the amount of anchor line or *rode* you let out between your bow and the anchor lying on the bottom. The number one mistake inexperienced sailors make when anchoring is not letting out enough anchor rode to keep the boat anchored. Shoot for a minimum of 7 feet of line for every 1 foot of depth. For example, if you're anchoring in 10 feet of water, you want at least 70 feet of line between the cleat on your bow and the anchor below. But when in doubt, let more out.

Like any good rule, this one has exceptions. Less scope is okay when

- You're just stopping for a short lunch and it's not windy.

- You're using a heavy anchor—the heavier the anchor, the less scope you need.

- You are using an all-chain rode, or a lot of chain attached to a rope rode.

When anchoring with an engine, you'd put the engine in reverse to move your boat backward as you pay out your rode. When anchoring under sail, wind or current eventually do the trick, and the boat lines up into the wind with the anchor rode stretched out ahead. In heavy current and light wind, the current direction takes over and the rode might stream off at an angle. That's okay. Lower your sails only after you're sure the anchor is holding.

If you're sailing in warm waters, you might want to go for a swim to check how the anchor is set on the bottom. An anchor can break free as the boat swings if the rode is caught in the *flukes* (the sharp points at the end of the anchor that are designed to dig into the bottom). The anchor can also break free if it catches on coral or something that could cause the rope to wear as the boat pivots with the wind. The flukes should be dug into the sand or mud or under something, such as a rock or ledge.

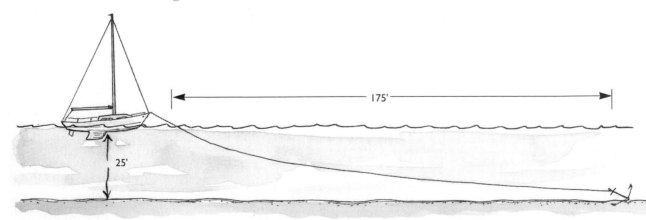

The recommended minimum amount of **scope** when anchoring is 7 feet for every foot of depth.

While anchored, be aware of your boat's relative distance from other boats and shore. Periodically check to make sure you're not *dragging* (the anchor is no longer hooked) and that a wind or current shift hasn't placed your boat in a vulnerable situation. If you're uncomfortably close to another boat or shore, proper sailing etiquette dictates that the last boat in moves first. In that case, be prepared to get your mainsail up to move around the harbor and find another spot. If you have to move, bring the anchor all the way aboard or right up to the bow so it can't bang into the hull and damage it.

Anchors are sized in relation to the size and weight of your boat. Some anchors hold better in rocky areas, others hold better in mud or sand, and few hold well in grass. Line and chain are purchased separately. All but the smallest anchors are usually attached to a length of galvanized chain with a shackle and pin. The pin is held firmly in place with seizing wire so the pin cannot come out. The chain is then attached to rope. The length of chain does two things:

- helps avoid chafe in the rope;
- provides extra holding power as it sits on the bottom.

Back to the dock under sail

Approach a dock slowly. You'll probably need at least your mainsail up to control your direction and speed.

If the wind's dead ahead, you can slow the boat down by *backing the main* (pushing it out against the wind). This is an easy maneuver on small boats, since the main and boom are not very big. Uncleat the mainsheet and let it run as you push the boom out perpendicular to the boat. At the same time, let the jib luff. Use your arms or body weight to keep the boom out there until the boat comes to a stop and starts moving backward. As the boat picks up momentum, you might want to let the boom swing back into the boat, allowing the mainsail to luff. It all depends on how much distance you have to go. To steer backward, push the tiller over to the port side of the boat to make the stern go to port, and over to the starboard side to make the stern go right. You might find it easier, at least at first, to face backward to steer backward. Some of the most seasoned skippers back a boat up this way. This is perfectly okay as long as someone is watching your bow, because it's swinging too. As the stern goes to port, the bow goes to starboard, and vice versa. If there are other boats or obstacles around, ask one of your crew to stand by in the bow with a fender.

If the wind is blowing onto the dock and you want to back into a slip under sail, when you're in position push the mainsail out against the wind and drift back. Secure a line from your bow to a cleat on the outboard end of the dock or a piling first, then attach a stern line to a cleat on the dock. When you've got your lines secured to the dock, release the mainsail, let it swing to the middle of the boat or in line with the wind, and get it down as quickly as you can. To learn more about how to cleat a line, see page 66.

Sailors are friendly folks, always willing to drop what they're doing and stand ready to take a line when a boat approaches. However, if no one is around, one of your crew needs to get on the dock to secure the boat. Allow the boat to get right up to the dock before anyone jumps. Long before you start the docking procedure, run through this checklist:

- Fenders placed along the side, positioned at the right height so they'll sit between your hull and the dock. (Put fenders on both sides if you are going into a narrow slip, or between a dock and another boat.)

- Docklines should be ready in the bow and stern, tied to a cleat and neatly coiled, and ready to toss or carry ashore—all led under lifelines, bow and stern pulpits, and any sheets lying on the deck.

- If you're not sure whether you'll have your port or starboard side to the dock, have your lines ready in the bow and the stern, and cleat them as soon as you do know.

Notice how I emphasize cleating docklines to the boat. It might seem silly, but too often someone will toss a line ashore and stand there holding it, and the tension on the line pulls it out of their hands as the boat continues moving! Sometimes the wind is working against you, pushing the boat away from the dock and making it nearly impossible to get a wrap around a cleat. If you start with the line secured to a cleat on the boat, you can always ease the line out or take more in later.

Cleating a dockline on the bow.

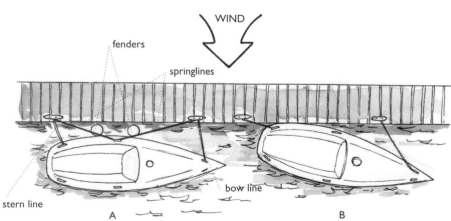

Springlines leading from the middle of the boat to cleats on the dock opposite the stern and bow keep the boat parallel to the dock and resting on fenders, with minimal fore-and-aft movement (**A**). Without springlines, the boat can sashay back and forth along the dock, and the stern (or bow) can swing into the dock (**B**), causing damage to the boat.

You also want extra lines leading from the middle of the boat. Attach a line to a cleat aft and lead it forward, and attach a line to a cleat in or near the bow and lead it back. These are *springlines*. See diagram on page 64. They will not only keep the boat from see-sawing back and forth along the dock, but they keep it parallel to the dock. Picture what can happen if the boat is tied only with a bow and stern line. If wind or current pushes you forward, the stern will swing in and hit the dock as the bow swings out. If wind or current pushes you backwards, the bow will hit the dock as the stern swings out.

If you dock stern-in, to keep from moving back into the dock or sea wall, first get a line from your bow to a piling or the dock. Then set a springline from the stern to a cleat or piling on the dock that is near or forward of the middle of your boat.

If you dock bow-in, get a line from the stern to a piling or the dock. Then secure another line from the bow to a cleat or piling that is near or aft of the middle of the boat to keep the bow from hitting the wall or perpendicular dock.

After you've tied your lines ashore, you can ease or tighten them to better situate the boat. Always check the final knots or cleats. Some kind helpers might not do the best job.

At a fixed dock (one that does not float up and down with the tide), you might have to allow for tidal changes. Take the time to adjust your fenders so they're between the boat and pilings, and between the hull and the dock.

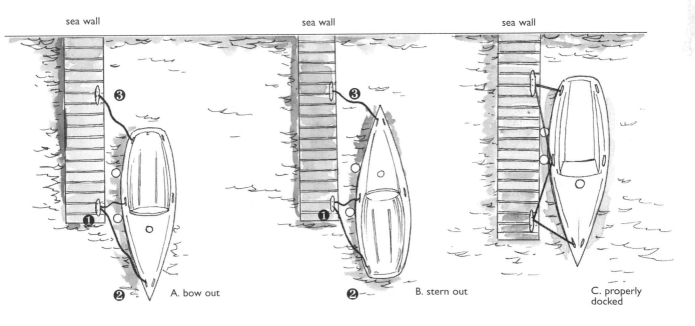

sea wall   sea wall   sea wall

A. bow out   B. stern out   C. properly docked

To avoid hitting a wall or dock when docking bow- or stern-in: tie a springline from the middle of your boat to a cleat at the end of the dock (1), then tie a line from bow (A) or stern (B) to the same cleat (2), and a third line from stern (A) or bow (B) to a cleat near the wall (3), then tighten lines as (C) to bring boat close to dock.

right way
to cleat

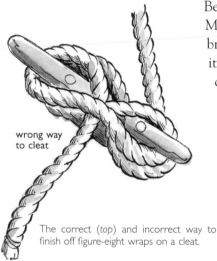

wrong way
to cleat

The correct (*top*) and incorrect way to finish off figure-eight wraps on a cleat.

Proper cleating

Boats and docks usually have cleats to hold lines in place. You can tie a knot through a cleat, or pass a loop over the two ends. The proper way to cleat, however, is to wrap the line in a figure-eight pattern around the cleat several times. Finish this off by twisting one loop and making sure the free end is lying underneath the final wrap. The free end must run in the same direction as the lines underneath it (see left).

How to throw a line

Before you toss a line ashore, cleat or tie one end to the boat. Make sure the line is led off the boat under the lifelines. Then bring the line back onto the boat, over the lifelines. Make sure it's coiled neatly (see Chapter 6 for more on coiling). Split the coil into two sections. Hold the outboard section (with the end you want someone to catch) in your throwing hand, and the tied end in your other hand. Leave about 3–5 feet of loose line in between. When you know you're close enough to the person who will catch your line, swing your throwing arm wide from behind and let the coils go, like a cowgirl.

You might want to put a loop in the end of the line you're tossing so it can be placed easily onto a cleat or mooring post. After your helper has secured the line ashore, take up the slack on the cleat on your boat.

The proper way to toss a line to shore. Coil the rope, hold half of the coils in one hand, placing the other half in your throwing hand (with 3–5 feet between) (1), then fling the coil to the helper ashore (2).

Using the iron genny

Sailors affectionately refer to auxiliary power on a sailboat as the iron genny. A lot of sailboats have outboard motors attached to the stern, or they have an inboard engine housed in a compartment on the boat. Many of you will continue the learning process on larger boats with cruising in mind, and you'll enjoy the luxury of going in and out of harbors and leaving mooring areas with the help of a generally reliable diesel or gasoline engine.

I think it's the "generally reliable" phrase that causes some women to have engine phobia. There are maintenance procedures to be followed, oil and water to be checked, gauges to read to make sure an engine is running properly. Don't think this is a "guy thing." You can take women-only workshops to learn how to care for and troubleshoot diesel engines.

Outboard motors

Outboard motors on sailboats are usually quite small, and they are used only for getting in and out of difficult marinas or when there's no wind and you've got to get back to shore. In most conditions, your boat will go faster under sail than powered by a small motor (a 6-hp motor is average). To start an outboard:

1. Make sure the gear lever is in neutral.

2. Open the choke lever or button.

3. Squeeze the bulb on the hose leading to the gas can a couple of times.

4. Open the throttle lever just a little and pull the starter cord (or there might be a starter key).

5. As soon as the engine engages, close the choke.

6. Push the throttle level back to the shift position, if the motor is running hard.

7. When ready to move forward under power, push the gear level to forward.

Steering by the handle on the outboard motor can be very difficult with a small motor. It's far easier to leave the engine in a fore-and-aft position and steer with your boat's tiller. To put the motor in reverse, bring the throttle back to shift first, then move the gear lever through neutral to reverse. To kill the engine, open the choke lever or button or turn off the key.

Inboard engines

Most inboard engines are powered by diesel fuel, which is safer than the gas-driven engines on some older cruising boats. If you do have a gas engine, it's very important to turn on the blowers to get combustible fumes out of the boat before starting the engine. To operate an inboard engine:

1.   Make sure the engine is in neutral. On some boats you may find a button (which should be out when the engine's in neutral) on the base of a lever that doubles as a throttle.

2.   Push the handle slightly forward to allow extra fuel to get the engine started.

3.   The starter motor of an inboard engine draws electricity from boat batteries in order to start. These must also be on before you turn a key.

4.   If there is an engine preheat button, hold it in for about 30 seconds.

5.   Turn the key to on. You should hear a buzzer or ringing noise. This indicates low oil pressure, which is natural when starting and stopping an engine. This is of concern only if the alarm comes on while the engine is running.

6.   When the engine engages, bring the throttle back to neutral.

7.   To put the engine in gear and move forward, push in the button on the throttle lever and slowly move the throttle forward.

8.   To go in reverse, bring the throttle back slowly, stop momentarily in neutral, then pull back to get the boat moving slowly backward.

Note that I keep emphasizing to shift gears slowly. If you ram your boat into reverse while it's at high revs in neutral, or while moving forward you shove the gear level from full ahead quickly to reverse without hesitating in neutral, it puts a tremendous strain on the transmission and propeller since they are forced to change direction at high revolutions. The same thing will happen if you go from reverse to forward quickly or at high revs. Before you ever put an engine in gear, make sure there are no lines dragging in the water that can get caught up in the propeller. If this happens, more than likely someone will have to go over the side and free them manually.

To stop an engine, after you're settled in:

1.   Make sure it's in neutral.

2.   Pull the engine stop button out. The alarm will sound again, indicating low oil pressure.

3.   Turn off the key, and the alarm will stop.

4.   Push the stop button back in or you won't be able to start the engine next time.

Anchoring under power

As you get your sails down and pull your anchor out, the engine should be on. Motor into the wind toward the spot where you want to drop the anchor; put the engine in neutral far enough in advance to allow the boat to drift to a dead stop. Then slowly lower the anchor into the water, making sure the rode is under the lifelines and any other lines it could get tangled in. When the anchor touches bottom, allow the boat to drift backward while the anchor rode runs out. Your engine is still in neutral.

When you think you have enough line out, put the engine in reverse and gently back down until the line feels taut. While you do this, watch a point on shore, or another boat, to make sure the anchor is set and your angle to this landmark is not changing. If the point on shore or the other boat seems to be moving forward, the anchor has not yet grabbed. When you're hooked, the angle to your reference point or object should not change.

While the boat is moving backwards, put your hand on the anchor line. If you feel steady pressure without vibration, you're probably hooked. If not, and the boat is still moving backwards, you'll feel vibration in the line indicating the anchor is moving with the boat. If you think your boat is dragging, you can let out some additional scope. But nine times out of ten, you'll need to pick up your anchor and start all over. Don't worry about what others might think. Your anchor might have found a grassy patch or ended up with chain or rope around a fluke so it can't grab properly.

To get the anchor up with an engine, motor very slowly toward the anchor as the bow person hauls the rode aboard. The bow person hauling the rode (or a helper) should point toward the direction the line is running off the boat, so you can steer toward the anchor. When the line is slack, put the boat in neutral and let the bow person bring the rest of the line and the anchor aboard.

"My first time bringing a boat into a dock, I was panicked—mouth dry, heart pumping hard—and then I remembered the drill: throttle back to near idle, take a deep breath, let the crew do their work, and come in real slow. It worked!"

—Kate Kerr, age 39

Docking with an engine

The principles of docking with an engine are the same as docking under sail, but the procedure gets a lot easier because you can get your sails down and folded (or *furled*) and your fenders and docklines out before you reach the dock. The main thing to remember is to power slowly as you approach the dock and put the engine in neutral before you get there. The boat's momentum will carry you the rest of the way. If you're going too fast, you might have to put the engine in reverse to slow down.

If you're heading into a slip with the wind on your nose, it should be relatively easy to glide in and get someone ashore with the docklines. If the wind is on your beam as you head in, you'll have to get your lines ashore quickly and compensate by using reverse gear to bring you closer to the dock. If the wind is pushing your beam onto the dock, you'll need to steer farther out as you approach and let the wind push you down.

All this is written very simply, but there's much more to the picture—wind strength, current, other boats around you. If you start cruising, you'll want to practice docking techniques while you're at the helm. One of my pet peeves is seeing a couple come into a marina with the man on the helm yelling orders (usually because he's coming in too fast), and the woman on the bow looking white-faced as she sees the dock approaching at breakneck speed.

Putting the boat to bed

Always leave your boat shipshape. Take the following steps to put your boat to bed:

1. If sails come off the boat, take them off and fold them, bag them, and store them out of sight.

2. When sails stay on, furl them neatly. Cover the sails left on the boom.

3. Coil the lines (see Chapter 6 for more information on coiling).

4. Place winch handles safely below or in their pockets in the cockpit.

5. Secure your halyards away from the mast. Otherwise, they make a racket! Secure them to a shroud base, the end of the boom, or another strong spot. Do this even if your mast is wood: a dull thumping can still be heard throughout the marina on a windy night.

Don't leave halyards attached to the heads of sails, even if you have them tied down, unless you're just making a daytime stop. Aside from looking bad, the sails can become untied in a bad blow, billow out over the boat, and eventually rip.

If you store sails ashore, disconnect all the outhauls and downhauls and loosen sheets before lowering the halyards. When your mainsail is down, tighten the boom with the mainsheet and boom vang. That way, the boom won't swing around while you pull the sail off or fold it. Raise the topping lift to get the boom out of the way. Remember to ease the mainsheet and boom vang just enough to allow the boom to be pulled up with the topping lift.

Folding sails off the boat. Starting at the foot, make accordion folds, then fold or roll the sail to fit in its bag, with the end you will need first next time on top (clew for main, tack for jib). Note how careful they are to avoid unnecessary creases in the sailcloth.

Many sailors leave their mainsails flaked on the boom and covered with a sun-resistant sail cover. The job of flaking (accordion-folding a sail), whether on or off the boom, works better with two people. If you are removing the sail completely, lay it across the boom or on the deck. Or, if you can, take it off the boat and lay it on the dock. With one person at the clew and one person at the tack, stretch the foot neatly and make your folds by each placing a hand about 2 feet up the leech and luff and bringing the same amount of cloth over to the foot. Continue to make these folds, stretching the cloth out as you go, until you get to the head. Be careful not to place a fold in the middle of any plastic windows. Then roll or fold the sail over from the tack end first, so the clew is on the outside when the sail is packed into the bag.

If you want to store the mainsail on the boom, make accordion folds in the same manner as when ashore (1), securing the folds with a sail tie (2). A sun-resistant sail cover (as seen on the boats in the background) provides needed protection.

If you leave the sail on the boom, loosen the outhaul to take the strain off and make the folds over the boom so that an equal amount of cloth (about 1 foot) hangs over each side. Stretch the cloth as you go. Sometimes the folds slip, and you must tie the outboard layers down before you finish. Then pass the head of the sail around the boom and cinch it tight with a *sail tie* (a sail tie is simply a length of webbing used to secure sails). Some sailors use a square knot for this (see page 109 for how to tie). I like to put a bowline in one end of the sail tie, pass the other end through the loop, pull tight, and secure it with a half-hitch. Bungee cords and regular line are also used to tie down sails.

Then, put your sail cover on and tie it in place with the toggles and lines provided, from gooseneck to outhaul. If you don't have a sun-resistant sail cover, you shouldn't leave your sail on the boom for more than a quick stop during the day because ultraviolet rays will eventually weaken the sailcloth.

On roller-furled jibs, sun-resistant cloth is sewn along the leech of the jib. This panel ends up on the outside when the jib is furled, and it protects the sail from ultraviolet rays. Rarely do you fool with the halyard of a roller-furled jib. Just leave the halyard in place and pull in on the furling line. Make sure your keep enough tension in the sheets to make a nice tight furl. Keep hauling in on the sheets until they've gone around the furled sail a couple of times. Coil and tie off the furling line. When you're done, put some tension on the jibsheets so they don't flail around in the wind.

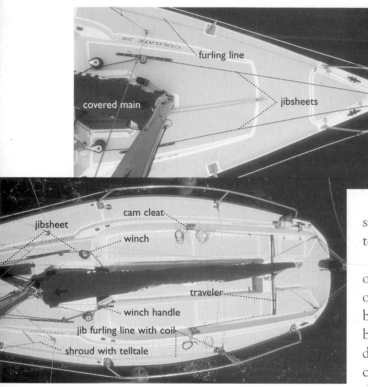

Two views of a boat put to bed, with roller-furled jib and covered mainsail. **Top:** Aerial view of the cockpit and deck from the mast looking forward shows furled jib with sheets leading aft through blocks on tracks to self-tailing winches on either side of the mast, furling line from drum at base of furled jib running back to cockpit along port side through blocks, and a covered mainsail stored on the boom. **Above:** Aerial view of the deck and cockpit from the mast looking aft shows jibsheet leading through blocks on tracks, winch handle stored in holder on port side of companionway, shrouds on either side of the mast with telltales indicating wind direction at dock, jib furling line along port side through blocks to coil hanging on lifelines just aft of last stanchion, stanchions and lifelines on both sides of boat, covered mainsail on boom, aft end of mainsheet running through blocks to traveler, and lines that adjust traveler running through block at either end forward to cam cleats in the middle of the cockpit.

If you remove the jib completely, take the knots out of the end of the sheets, but leave them attached at the clew end if you like. Lay the foot of the sail along the deck, or on the dock ashore. With one person at each end of the foot, make the accordion folds. Be careful not to fold any plastic windows. Place the sheets neatly over the sail and fold or roll the sail in from the clew end first, leaving the tack on top. Then bag the sail, and you're almost done.

Coil all the halyard ends and tie them off or hang the coils over a cleat. Tie down the tiller, or tighten up the wheel, so the rudder can't slosh back and forth with current and ripples made by boats going by. Check your fenders, mooring, or docklines to make sure any knots you made won't come untied. If you sail in salt water, hose down the boat with fresh water if at all possible to get the salt off and keep corrosion to a minimum.

Boats with cabins have hatch boards with locks to close the companionway and keep the boat secure. If you have instruments attached to a battery, make sure they're turned off. The boat is now shipshape, and you can leave with a profound sense of accomplishment. You've learned a lot. At times, it might have seemed daunting. But it's already starting to gel—and you know that the time you spend learning now all adds up to confident gratification later on.

What is it about sailing that keeps us coming back? "The sense of freedom, peace, and exhilaration—the accomplishment of being very good at it," says Stephanie Argyris. "The pleasure of being outdoors and on the water, mastering sailing skills and knowledge," says Deborah Loeff. "Just feeling the wind, hearing the silence," says Jane Candella.

Chapter 5

USING THE WIND

You know how to get underway, enjoy a little sailing, and return home. The next step is to learn how sailboats interact with the wind and why they perform differently in various conditions.

• •

"**S**ome fear the wind at first, then learn to love it and the exhilaration of being one with the wind and water."

—Stephanie Argyris, age 46

IDENTIFYING WIND DIRECTION

• •

The wind is invisible, but there are ways to see its path. A flag or smokestack on land can tell you where the wind is blowing from, and how hard. If the flag's straight out, it's windy; if it's angling down, it's light. Other sailboats are another key: Soon you'll learn to tell the breeze direction by looking at another boat's point of sail.

True wind

If the boat is dead in the water (no sails up, or not moving because the sails are luffing), the wind direction you feel is the *true* (actual) direction. Move your face slowly from side to side and stop when you feel the wind flowing past your face equally on both sides. The direction you're facing is the true wind direction. Sometimes it helps to close your eyes as you do this.

Many boats have a *masthead fly*, which is perched at the very top of the mast and swings like a wind vane. Again, with the boat at a standstill, look aloft and see where it's pointing to find your true wind direction. The larger the boat, the more apt it is to have wind instruments in the cockpit. Connected by wire to the vane at the top of the mast, these instruments measure wind direction and strength.

Another way to find the true wind is by reading your *telltales*. These are pieces of yarn (old cassette tape works well, too) that you tie to your shrouds and backstay so you can read the wind direction.

Apparent wind

When the boat is moving through the water, with or without the sails up, the wind you feel is the *apparent wind*. This is a blend of true wind direction and boat speed. You feel this wind more when you're close-hauled or on a close reach, because you're still sailing toward the wind.

Telltales can be tied to shrouds and backstay or placed at intervals along the luff of the jib. They are usually made of old pieces of yarn, although cassette tape material works well, too.

SETTING YOUR SAILS UPWIND AND DOWNWIND

The direction the wind is blowing in relation to your boat determines how you trim your sails. To gauge how well your sails are set, place telltales at intervals along the luff to show airflow as it passes over the outside and inside of the sail.

Sailing upwind

If the jib is set properly when you're sailing close-hauled, both the inside telltale and the outside telltale will flow straight back. If you start to *head up*, and you sail too close to the wind direction for your current sail trim, the inside telltale starts to flutter. (To review heading up and falling off, see Chapter 3, "Taking a Sailboat Through Its Paces," page 49.) If you *fall off* too far, the outside telltale flutters. To maximize your speed upwind, steer by the telltales and keep them flowing equally over both sides of the jib.

However, if you need to change course while you're sailing upwind, or if the wind shifts, you can trim your sails to your new course. If the wind isn't flowing correctly over the jib and the outside telltale is fluttering, ease the jib out. If the inside telltale is fluttering, trim the jib in. Do this sail trimming in small increments: It doesn't take much to affect trim. Kim Auburn made up a ditty to help her remember how to trim to the telltales: When the outers flutter, ease out; when the inners flutter, trim in.

When you trim your mainsail for a close-hauled course, the main should be as close to the centerline of the boat as possible without causing it to luff. Sometimes you alter this trim for sea conditions and wind strength, as you'll learn later in the book. But the general rule for upwind sailing is to trim in both sails as tight as possible, while still maintaining smooth airflow.

When both main and jib are trimmed in tight, a slot is created between the jib and mainsail. Air moves faster as it's funneled through this narrow area. Its pressure is increased and, as a result, so is your speed and efficiency.

Sometimes the main luffs slightly when the air flowing off the leech of the jib hits the luff of the main. That's okay, as long as you maintain your speed in the direction you want to travel in. However, if you feel the boat is slowing down or acting sluggish, and there's more than a slight softness along the luff, your main is probably *backwinded* (luffing excessively from air flowing off the jib), indicating that the slot between the jib and main is not funneling air efficiently. To cure this and increase your speed, first try trimming in the mainsail and making it flatter. If this doesn't work, ease the jib just enough to calm down the luff. (See Chapter 7 for more about trimming the main and jib for maximum efficiency.)

> "**I** was at the helm and a sudden storm came up, with terrific wind. My instructor said, 'Jean, just keep doing what you're doing. It's perfect.' I relaxed and concentrated on sailing. It was perfect!"
>
> —Jean Webster, age 57

Sailing off the wind

When sailing close-hauled, the crew trims the sails to create an efficient slot between the mainsail and jib; then, unless the wind direction changes, the driver steers up or down to keep the telltales flowing smoothly. If adjustments are needed to maintain speed, you usually adjust the jib first. On a reach, the driver maintains the course she wants to sail, and the crew adjusts the sails in and out to keep the telltales flowing smoothly. On this point of sail, the jib and main receive equal attention.

Use the same guidelines to trim your jib to your course as described for upwind sailing. The mainsail on a reach is also adjusted in and out to maintain the proper course for the wind direction. However, it's a little harder to judge exactly where the main should be set, and it's easier to *over trim* (pull the sail in too tight). A mainsail let out too far will definitely luff, but if it's in too tight you might not see the problem without experimenting. Ease the main out a little at a time until the luff just starts to flutter, then bring it back enough to stop that luffing. You can also watch for increases or decreases in boat speed, if you have instruments aboard that tell you how fast you're sailing.

Sailing downwind

As you sail downwind, you are traveling with the wind. The apparent wind speed and your boat's speed might be close to equal, and it might seem as if there's no wind at all.

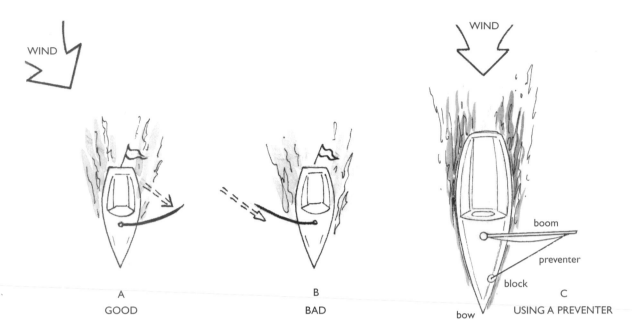

Sailing by the lee: Boat A is safely set up for downwind sailing. The mainsail is out to port and the wind (look at flag) is coming over the starboard side. Boat B is sailing by the lee. Notice how the wind is hitting the back side of the sail. This could cause an uncontrolled jibe on Boat B. To hold the boom out on a run dead downwind: tie a preventer from a point near the end of the boom to a block near the bow as shown in Boat C. Remember to remove the preventer before you jibe or try to head up.

To determine if your mainsail is set correctly for the direction of the wind, look at the flag on your stern (if you have one) or the telltales on your backstay. In the diagram above, if your mainsail is out over the port side of the boat, and the flag or telltales are flowing at an angle toward the mainsail from anywhere on your starboard side, you're fine. But if the mainsail is over the starboard side of the boat, and the wind is flowing toward it from the starboard side, the wind will hit the outer, back side of the mainsail. This is called *sailing by the lee*. On this point of sail, your boat is on the verge of a jibe—and if you're not careful, you could easily have an uncontrolled jibe.

In this situation, you want to shift the sail safely to the other side in a controlled jibe, as soon as possible. When you're sailing dead downwind, the mainsail should be as far out as possible—sometimes even resting against the spreaders and shrouds. An uncontrolled jibe can be dangerous because the boom will swing across the boat before crew is set up to handle this maneuver. When the boom has such a long way to go, an uncontrolled jibe—especially on larger boats—packs a lot of power! If someone is standing in the way of the boom when it swings, it could be trouble. (You'll learn how to make a controlled jibe later in this chapter, in "Maneuvering Downwind," page 82.)

You can rig a *preventer* to help hold the boom out as you cruise downwind. To do this, attach a line onto the boom, near the outboard end, and lead that line to a block positioned along the rail of the deck and toward the bow. The preventer keeps the boom out over the side of the boat as long as you stay on that jibe. If the wind shifts, it should be removed and the boat should be jibed.

MAKING THE BOAT REACT TO YOU

A sailboat moves smoothly when everyone on the boat understands the job they need to do. So let's see what it takes to actually execute sailing maneuvers, such as a tack, a jibe, falling off, and heading up.

"Maneuvers like tacking and jibing are easy concepts for women to learn, because we think through the steps."

—Ginny Worcester, age 40

If you're sailing alone, which is called sailing singlehanded, and there are no other boats in your vicinity, you obviously don't have to announce your plans. If other boats are around and a change in your heading could put you close to another boat or in its path, it's common sense and courtesy to state your intention and watch for acknowledgment. More than likely, you'll be sailing with friends and family aboard who take an active part. Steering is just part of the equation in a sailing maneuver. Tell your crew what you are doing so they can prepare and work together as a team.

At first, in a tack, you might have a tendency to rush: Throw the helm over quickly and spin the boat through the wind. In most cases, the crew and the sails just can't keep up, and the boat will slow down or stop. When you're at the helm, remember these three phrases: sensitive touch, smooth moves, slow down.

Maneuvering upwind

When you sail upwind on a beat, each time you tack you move the boat through the wind and move the sails from one side of the boat to the other. Each tack will get smoother and smoother with practice.

"Maneuvers like tacking and jibing are easy concepts for women to learn, because we think through the steps," says instructor Ginny Worcester.

What are these steps in a tack? You're at the helm, steering close-hauled on starboard and you want to tack to port. Call out, "Ready about?" to let the crew know you are preparing for a tack. They take their positions and answer back, "Ready."

What are these positions? Most of the physical work in tacking involves the jib. Both sails are over the port side of the boat. The *active* jibsheet is presently controlling the jib, wrapped around the port winch and cleated. One crew moves to the port side of the boat and uncleats the active jibsheet. She simply holds it and doesn't take it off the winch drum. Another crew stays on the starboard side, puts one or two wraps of the *inactive* jibsheet around the winch. Then she takes up the slack in the line by pulling any excess into the cockpit without putting pressure on the clew of the sail. The person on the mainsheet stands by ready to grab the sheet in case it comes free, in case the wind shifts or strengthens, or in case you decide to fall off after completing the tack (in which case she'll ease the mainsail out).

Before you tack, pick a point the boat will be heading at when the tack is completed. You should be sailing at about 45 degrees from the direction of the wind. When you tack you should end up about 45 degrees on the other side of the wind, or a total of 90 degrees from your heading.

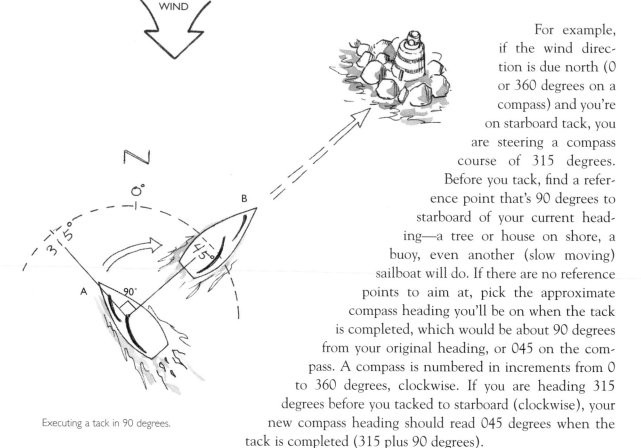

Executing a tack in 90 degrees.

For example, if the wind direction is due north (0 or 360 degrees on a compass) and you're on starboard tack, you are steering a compass course of 315 degrees. Before you tack, find a reference point that's 90 degrees to starboard of your current heading—a tree or house on shore, a buoy, even another (slow moving) sailboat will do. If there are no reference points to aim at, pick the approximate compass heading you'll be on when the tack is completed, which would be about 90 degrees from your original heading, or 045 on the compass. A compass is numbered in increments from 0 to 360 degrees, clockwise. If you are heading 315 degrees before you tacked to starboard (clockwise), your new compass heading should read 045 degrees when the tack is completed (315 plus 90 degrees).

Everyone's ready. Call out, "Hard alee" and push the tiller slowly away from the direction you intend to go. The *lee* side of a boat is the side that's away from the wind, the side of the boat the wind hits last. The *windward* side is where the wind hits first. Hard alee indicates you're pushing the tiller away from the wind to the lee side. Some people say, "Helms alee." Others just say, "Tacking."

As soon as you give the command, the crew on the active jibsheet takes a wrap or two off the winch drum without letting the sheet slip. The crew on the other side is ready to pull in, with no more than two wraps around the drum of the free winch.

Winch drums generally turn clockwise, and your wraps around the drum should also be clockwise. If in doubt, just spin the drum to see which direction it spins in before wrapping the sheet around it. It's futile to try to trim in when the wraps are opposite the turning direction of the drum: nothing happens!

To take wraps off an active winch, to ease a sheet or get ready for a tack, use your free hand as a brake, pressing against the coils around the drum to hold them in place.

If there's a lot of wind, or you're uncertain you can control the load on the winch, don't remove any wraps. If the remaining wraps slip around the drum and get away from you, it could

Above: The proper way to ease a sheet, using your free hand as a brake. **Right:** Trimming sail using your upper body strength, and a self-tailing winch.

be dangerous to interfere. The load on the sheet is so heavy that you could get serious rope burn, or your hand can be pulled into the winch and get caught in the line. Be careful.

As the boat turns through the wind, the jib will begin to luff. At that point, the boat is turning head-to-wind. This is the optimal moment to throw the old sheet completely off the winch and trim in the new one. As the port sheet is released, the starboard sheet is pulled in. To get the line off the winch quickly, pull straight up. Before too much tension is felt on the new sheet, with one hand put more wraps around the starboard winch and pull hard. Your crewmate can now jump over and help you get the sail in the rest of the way. She pulls the free end of the sheet coming off the drum, while you crank the handle in the winch to trim the sail in. If tension isn't maintained in the free end, you can crank your heart out and nothing will happen. The coils around the winch will just sit there while the drum turns.

A winch handle has a sprocket on one end that fits in the top of the drum and a perpendicular hand grip at the other. It is usually kept in a pocket near the winch and placed in the top of the drum after you have placed your extra wraps around the drum and can no longer get the sheet in by hand. If you put the handle in before it's needed, it will free-spin dangerously as the drum spins. Also, when you need to place more wraps on the drum, it will be in the way. If not locked in place, a handle can fall out and possibly go overboard. And you don't want it in the way if you need to let a sheet out in a hurry. When not needed for trimming, keep the winch handle in a safe spot nearby and not in the top of the winch.

When you pull a jibsheet, pull with your thumbs toward you. This makes you use your biceps, as Offshore's Operations Director Michelle Boggs points out. If you pull with your thumbs toward the sail, you'll use your back.

Cranking a winch is easy if you position your body weight properly over the winch. If you

Above: The wrong way to put wraps on a winch shows fingers holding the wrap. As the line leading off drum is tightened, those fingers can be easily caught and injured.
Right: The correct way to put wraps on a winch using one hand to circle the drum as line slides through fingers.

stay level with the handle, all the work will come from your arm, and it's easy to tire. Stand up over the winch, grab the handle in both hands, and put your whole upper body into it. You'll be amazed how fast the sail comes in and how little stress you'll feel. Some big boats with large winches have handles two people can crank together, so the sail comes in that much faster.

There's a right and wrong way to put wraps on a winch. Use one hand and rapidly circle the winch, allowing the line to slip through your hand while maintaining a little tension. Never hold a loop of the line with any fingers of your other hand between the line and the drum of the winch.

Why do you start with only one or two wraps? When there's no tension on the line and too many wraps on the winch, the coils don't stay neatly in place and they can *override*, or crisscross, each other. When pressure is put on the line leading to the winch as the sail fills, the tangled wraps tighten up unmercifully and you can't pull the sail in or let it out. To cure this Chinese wrap, as sailors sometimes call it, you'll have to tack back and get the tension off that sheet. If you can't tack back (because there's an obstruction) or you don't want to tack back, rig up a line to take the tension off. The latter is complicated and time consuming. It's best to avoid the problem altogether.

Override on a winch. When too many wraps are placed on the drum before there's enough tension, the sheets get fouled, leaving them unable to be eased or trimmed.

Now let's get back to steering. Throughout this maneuver, the helmsman watches the sails too. At the point they pass to the other side of the boat, start to bring the tiller back toward the center of the boat—but not all the way. Move in front of the tiller to the new high side of the boat. As the sail is trimmed in, complete the tack by steering the boat to your new heading.

Always face forward when changing sides, slipping the tiller from one hand to the other behind you as you side-step across the boat. This keeps you alert to what's going on both on the boat and around you. And when crossing the boat during a tack, it's a lot easier if you time your move to coincide with those few moments when the boat is flat.

If your crew is having trouble bringing in the jib (which can happen when you get a little out of sync, or in heavy air), you can help by heading up toward the wind ever so slightly, for just a moment. This reduces the pressure on the sail and allows your crew to pull or crank in quickly. This is called giving the crew a luff. Care must be taken not to go past head-to-wind (back through the wind, the way you came) or you'll end up having to tack back to your old heading and start all over again.

A KINDER CLEAT

Small cleats used all over the boat reduce the need for larger old-fashioned hardware, which can slow down maneuvers and—if you sit on one or bump into one—can also give you nasty bruises (or what sailors call boat bites).

A cam cleat is a smaller, low-profile cleat. It acts like a set of spring-loaded jaws with teeth. To release, pull the line up (or down, depending on how the cleat is positioned) and completely out of the jaws. To hold the line in place, pull it through the cleat while there's still tension on it. To trim a line in a cam cleat without removing it, simply pull straight through, not up (or down).

Left to right: Typical mainsheet block leading to a cam cleat. Cam cleat in use. Cam cleats, blocks, and rope clutches—all used for various halyards and reefing lines running from mast and boom to cockpit area.

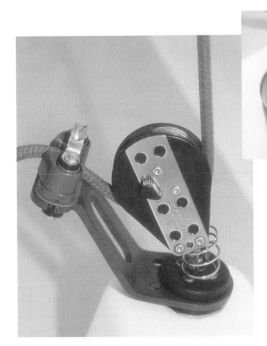

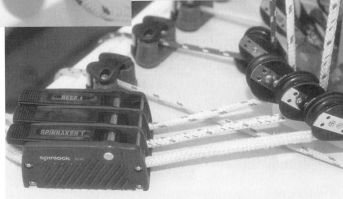

Common tacking problems

The following is a list of common problems you might encounter as you learn to tack.

- Tacking too fast (spinning the boat) can stop a sailboat dead by spilling the wind out of the sails or pounding the boat into a wave.

- An incomplete tack occurs because you pulled the tiller back amidships before the boat crossed through the wind completely. If the boat isn't turned far enough, the sails don't fill sufficiently, and they'll keep on luffing. In this case, the boat slows down, stops (goes in irons), might start to drift backwards, and can eventually fall off in a direction you don't want to go in. If you end up in irons, back the jib and ease the mainsail to get underway again. As soon as the boat starts to move, pull the mainsail back in to its close-hauled position and trim your jib properly. The boat should gain momentum as the wind pressure increases in the sails.

- When you tack, you might end up on a reach rather than a close-hauled course if you don't bring the tiller back in time to offset the bow's momentum. If this happens, gradually trim your sails and steer to a close-hauled course.

- A jib will back on its own if the old sheet is not released in time, or if it is left cleated and not released properly. This forces the bow down and keeps you from bringing the boat up to a close-hauled course.

Maneuvering downwind

You're at the helm, sailing downwind, and want to jibe. Say, "Prepare to jibe!" Everyone takes their positions. When they're ready, they answer, "Ready!"

If you're worried about an accidental jibe, watch your jib. If it starts to dance (tries to switch sides because it's blanketed by the main), remember the phrase, "tiller toward the boom to avoid doom." Do that, and your boat will head up and avoid an accidental jibe.

As the driver, your responsibilities are to watch the direction the boat is going, keep it on course, and to make sure you give the crew enough warning to prepare for the jibe.

In preparation for the jibe, the person on the mainsheet pulls the main in, bringing the sail near the middle of the boat. If the sail was all the way out to the spreaders, this might take a little time.

You might or might not have a jib up if you're sailing dead downwind. Some sailors like to roll the jib up or take it down if it's completely blanketed and flopping back and forth. But for now, let's assume the jib is up and on the same side as the mainsail as you prepare to jibe.

When the mainsail is trimmed in to your satisfaction, say, "Jibe ho" (or "Jibing") and start to turn the boat. At the point the mainsail crosses the boat, the crew on the mainsheet lets the sheet run out on the other side, all the while keeping it under control. Everyone should take care not to get caught in the sheet as it runs out, and duck as the boom goes over.

On the jib, one crew releases the active jibsheet, but keeps a little tension on the sheet so the sail doesn't cross the boat around the outside of the forestay. The crew on the opposite jibsheet hauls in the new sheet. On some boats, like a Colgate 26, one crew can handle both jibsheets.

A dead downwind jibe doesn't require much change in course, sometimes just a few degrees.

Controlling a jibe on *Sirocco*. Hauling in on the mainsheet to center the boom before the boat jibes.

Common jibing problems

When you're learning to jibe, you might encounter some of the following problems.

- If you push the tiller over too fast in a jibe, the boom can fly across the boat too quickly and out of control.

- If you don't push the tiller over far enough on a jibe, the boom will just hang there, waiting for the wind to catch it and bring it across.

- If you push the tiller too far over on a jibe, you might start going in circles.

How to do a reach-to-reach jibe

You might not always be sailing dead downwind when you want to jibe. Sometimes you might want to go from a reach on port tack to a reach on starboard tack. This is called a reach-to-reach jibe. On a reach, the jib and mainsail are equally important and are handled the same way as they are when tacking.

During a reach-to-reach jibe, if you intend to keep roughly the same angle to the wind as on the original jibe, you may allow the mainsheet to just swing over without tending it.

On a close reach, the boat might be heeled over at an angle like it is when you are close-hauled. Here, crew weight becomes very important: you want to get to the high side of the boat as quickly as possible to settle it down and get back in the groove after you jibe.

Changing course without changing tacks

Sometimes when you're sailing along, you want to change course without tacking or jibing. Or the wind might shift, causing you to change the trim of your sails to stay on the same heading.

Heading up

If the wind *lifts* you, it shifts and allows you to head up closer to the wind; just turn the boat toward the wind. You'll notice a lift when the jib's leeward telltales (on the back side of the sail) start to flutter, but the sail still looks fine. As you turn toward the wind, both telltales will line up and flow aft again.

If you head up without a wind shift, both the main and jib will start to luff if you don't adjust them. Trim both sails in as you turn upwind.

Remember the word *toward*: When you head up, you want to head *toward* the wind, so push the tiller *toward* the sail.

"Heading up!" is the command you call out. It describes the technique you use to steer anywhere from dead downwind to close-hauled while staying on the same tack. If your boat's bow continues to point closer and closer to the direction the wind is coming from, you'll eventually have to tack if you keep turning the boat in the same direction.

Remember, the sails are a sailboat's engine. You want them to be as efficient as possible to achieve optimal performance. That's why you constantly watch the sails and ease them out or trim them in for the direction you're headed. The lighter and smaller the boat, the more immediate effect trimming has. In dinghy racing, boats sometimes hover behind the starting line (an imaginary line that extends between a buoy and a boat) with sails luffing or eased out. When a gun goes off, they pull in their sails and dart forward upwind. On larger and heavier boats, it might take a while to feel the boat accelerate in response to sail adjustments.

Falling off

In the previous section, we ended the process of heading up by tacking. If you keep turning the boat in the same direction, once you're through your tack you'll have to ease the sails and fall off, or bear away.

Remember the word *away*: When falling off or bearing *away*, you want to turn *away* from the wind, so bring the tiller *away* from the mainsail.

As you fall off, move the tiller slowly away from your desired direction and start to ease both the jibsheet and the mainsheet. The mainsail can make or break this maneuver, particularly in heavy air when you're heeled far over and the rudder is near the surface. If it's not eased, you won't be able to fall off. The mainsail will only force the boat to heel farther and farther, and the rudder will lose its effectiveness. Eventually the boat will *round up* toward the wind.

Failure to ease the mainsheet quickly in heavy air as a boat turns downwind has caused many a collision—particularly when one boat tries to pass behind, or *duck*, another and can't turn to do so.

To prepare to fall off, say "Falling off" or "Prepare to ease." Give the trimmers time to get into position, uncleat their sheets, and watch the luffs of the sails as the boat starts to turn.

What will you see if the sails are not eased? If the boat is turned away from the wind and the sails are not eased, the wind will eventually stop flowing over the back side (the leeward side) of the sail, and the telltales will flutter or hang limp. The sails will not luff, but the boat will start to slow down. The sails are stalled. Easing them to their correct trim will get you back up to speed. Depending on the strength of the wind, the boat will also heel more and more until the sails are eased.

When sails are trimmed in flat in too much wind (particularly the mainsail), the boat heels farther and farther—and is said to be **overpowered**—bringing the rudder out of the water and making it ineffective as the helmsperson tries to steer down. Solution: ease the mainsheet (your biggest sail) quickly first. In this case the boat has a spinnaker up, too, with large sail area, which must also be eased.

Sailing without a rudder

Although it's highly unlikely you'll ever lose your rudder, learning to steer without one is a good exercise. To practice, tie the rudder amidships (in the middle of the boat) and ignore it. With one person on the mainsheet and another on the jibsheets, ease the jib and trim the main. The boat will head up toward the wind. To reverse this, or fall off, ease the main and trim the jib.

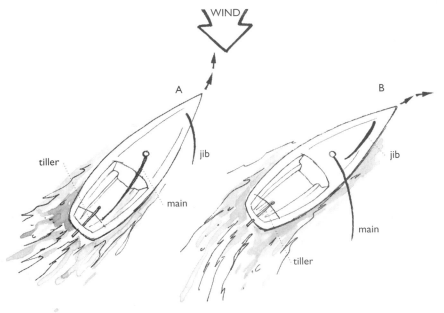

To practice steering without the use of the rudder, tie your tiller amidships. To head up (**A**), ease the jib and trim in the main. To fall off (**B**), trim in the jib and ease the main.

extra safety line through the grommet and around the boom, using a square knot or a half-hitch with a slip knot. If the reef line breaks at this point, the safety line will keep the sail from opening up and, in a domino effect, causing the rest of the reef points along the boom to break away.

Reefing the headsail

If you have a roller-furling genoa, you can reduce your headsail area by rolling it up part way until you feel the boat is balanced (it has less heel and is moving calmly) for the wind and wave conditions. To reef from the cockpit, have one crew pull in on the reefing line that runs around the sail's drum. Another crew simultaneously eases the jibsheet. There will be a lot of pressure in the sail and on that jibsheet, so take just enough wraps off the jib winch to ease without the sheet getting away from you. Remember to use your hand as a brake.

If you don't have a roller-furling system, you'll probably have to take down your headsail or change to a smaller one, depending on your sail inventory. To get it down quickly, someone has to lower the halyard while another crew pulls down on the jib and makes sure it stays aboard the boat. Tie the jib securely in a bundle to the forestay or take it off and throw it in the cockpit or below. On small boats, the jib should drop fairly quickly. On larger boats with big genoas, several crew will need to pull it on deck and keep it out of the water.

No one wants to have to go up on the foredeck in bad conditions. But if you must, take safety precautions—wear a life vest and use a safety harness at all times while on deck.

Other options for depowering

You might be out there alone or with inexperienced crew. Or you might be sailing a boat that doesn't have sails you can reef. In this case you can ease your mainsail to avoid excessive heeling, or you can take down your main and sail under jib alone. If you sail under main alone, you probably won't be able to *point* well (keep the boat on your desired heading), and you'll end up slipping sideways. Neither of these methods is very efficient. The best plan might be to find a spot to anchor and wait out the storm.

In heavy air, if you want a rest, if you can't reef, and if you don't want to anchor, you can *heave-to*. Heaving-to is a method where you work the jib against the main, which basically causes the boat to tread water and stay in one area. To do this, trim the jib to windward (on the wrong side of the boat) and flatten the mainsail, bringing it as close to centerline as possible. I've never found heaving-to particularly comfortable, though some racing sailors swear by it for a quick lunch between starts. Personally, I'd rather take turns steering around under main alone while the others eat.

In very stormy weather, this technique can be used to hover around a small area.

WIND

To heave-to: Trim the jib to windward and the mainsail in flat.

WHEN YOU GO AGROUND

Sooner or later, you'll experience going aground. While it's embarrassing, going aground is seldom life threatening.

If you sail a centerboard boat, the minute you touch ground you can pull up the board and sail away. Keelboats are much harder to get off. The first rule is to try to turn the boat and go out the same way you came in. You might not know the shape of the reef or sand bar you're on; but you do know that when you touched bottom, there was deep water behind you.

Immediately get everyone over to the leeward side to heel the boat. Trim the sails in tight, and try rocking the boat. Get body weight out as far as you safely can; try hanging onto a shroud while standing on the edge of the boat. As the keel raises up, you should feel the boat break free.

If this doesn't work, try to push off with a long paddle, boat hook, or spinnaker pole—although with a soft bottom, these will probably sink into the mud or sand.

On a small boat—if all else fails, and you're confident you can climb back aboard easily—get in the water and push the boat off. Before you leave the boat, however, loosen the sheets so the boat can't sail away. Maintain a firm hold so the boat doesn't get away from you when it breaks free. With help you can rotate the bow toward the direction you came from, with one person pushing the stern and another pushing the bow from the opposite side.

On a larger boat, and sometimes on smaller ones, the solution might be to *kedge off*. If you have a dinghy, use it to take an anchor, tied to the bow of the grounded boat, out as far as you can and drop it. Then come back aboard and, using a winch, keep tightening up on the anchor rode until the boat breaks free. To kedge off a small boat, you'll probably need to swim the anchor out the length of its rode. It generally doesn't do any good to try to throw it out: you just won't get it far enough to pull the boat off. Always wear a life vest—whether you use the dinghy or swim the anchor out, no matter how good a swimmer you are.

Someone might come along and offer to tow you off or help you heel over farther by pulling on a halyard. Don't use the halyard on a small boat; you could break your mast. If you do get help, there are two things you must consider: will there be a charge for this service, and will the other party claim salvage on your boat?

Assuming you are not in any danger and have time to negotiate, ask first if there will be a charge and how much. Then give the other party a line from your boat instead of accepting one from them. Why? There have been cases where, under Admiralty Law, the rescuer has successfully claimed salvage (ownership) of the boat it helped.

Make sure you use a line strong enough to take the strain, and tie it with a bowline or many half-hitches to a cleat in your bow, under your bow pulpit if you have one (see pages 106–113 about knots). Then, ask the helpful party to slowly start moving away from you. Stay away from the tied line, in case it snaps. When you're clear, motion the boat to slow down. When there's slack in the line, have them release the line so you can pull it back aboard your boat. This assumes you have had your sails up the entire time and are already sailing. If, for some reason, you took your sails down, have them ready to go. Before you cast off, get them up and drawing.

If you've tried everything and can't get off, you can call one of several towing firms. Boat Tow/U.S. and Sea Tow are both located on most U.S. waterways, and they accept credit cards. Be prepared, however, for a big bill. Boat Tow is part of BOAT/U.S., a national membership organization that also offers towing insurance.

Groundings can usually be avoided, especially if you're navigating constantly: checking your chart, allowing for current and leeway, staying aware of any obstructions and shallow water. (You'll learn more about navigation in Chapter 8.)

On one of our graduate cruises in Maine, our four boats anchored comfortably one afternoon and settled down to enjoy our evening cocktails with lobster bought earlier in the day. During the night, when the tide ebbed, a boat anchored to starboard of us—sitting closer to an outcropping of rocks—quietly went aground while everyone was asleep. Because of the rocks and the damage that could be done to the boat if we attempted to pull her off, we all waited around until the tide came back in. Embarrassed but unscathed, they floated off. Fortunately, there was little wind and the waters were calm.

On another occasion, we were anchored for lunch near shore off Hilton Head Island. The tide went out and we settled into the mud. No one was around to grab a tow, and our efforts to heel the boat and then kedge off were hopeless. So we waited the tide out and sailed back in, many hours later.

Both these situations could have easily been avoided by being more aware, checking our charts and tide tables, and thinking ahead. Be aware of tidal changes and take care not to sail or anchor too close to shore. When you anchor, make sure you will not go aground when the tide goes out, and you won't be forced into shallow water if the wind shifts.

As you get more experienced and adventurous in sailing, you might start cruising in exotic locations where there are coral reefs (which we love for snorkeling, but not for sailing!). Don't sail toward or near known reefs into the setting or rising sun. You want the sun behind you or directly overhead so you can see the bottom and pick out the darker colored heads of coral reefs.

CREW-OVERBOARD RECOVERY

In a good sailing course, you'll practice crew-overboard recovery procedures repeatedly. When you're out sailing around for pleasure later on, use these techniques to keep both you and your crew alert. There are several methods acknowledged by both our national sailing authority and the authorities of other countries. Two methods are described in this section.

No matter which method you use, always have a buoyant cushion available to throw overboard to the victim. Make sure that the minute a person goes overboard, one person's sole duty is to keep her eyes on the swimmer and feed information back to the driver.

LifeSling method

A widely accepted overboard retrieval method uses a LifeSling—a buoyant sling carried in a case that mounts on your stern pulpit. It's easily accessible, ready for deployment, and attached to the boat by a long, floating line.

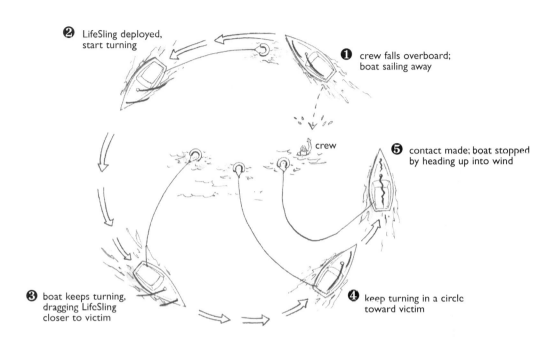

Crew-overboard recovery with a LifeSling. When the person falls overboard (**1**), deploy the LifeSling from the stern (**2**), while starting to turn the boat. Keep turning to draw the LifeSling closer to the person in the water (**3, 4**). As soon as contact is made (**5**), turn the bow into the wind and stop.

1.   The moment someone falls overboard, assuming that person is conscious and able to grab hold, throw the LifeSling over the side.

2.   Sail the boat in ever-tightening circles, being careful not to run over the line attached to the LifeSling.

3.   Instruct the victim to grab the line and work her way back to the LifeSling.

4.   Just as she reaches the sling, stop the boat by turning it directly into the wind; lower the jib if possible, or let it luff along with the main.

5.   At this point, everyone focuses on getting her back aboard.

6.   Get the jib down on deck quickly and push it out of the way; clip the freed halyard to a lifeline until you need it (see step 8).

7.   Using a jibsheet winch, pull her in the LifeSling to the stern quarter of the boat by cranking in on the attached line.

8.   When she's alongside but still in the water, cleat the line coming off the winch, attach one end of a block-and-tackle arrangement to the freed jib halyard and the other end to the sling, and haul her on deck.

If you plan to use a LifeSling, practice in all conditions to make sure you can handle the boat and get the person aboard. If you're left alone on the boat, the rescue is not easy but entirely possible—as has been proven in tests with only one woman left aboard. Remember, always wear a life vest and safety harness attached safely to lines aboard if you're on deck in heavy weather, which is when most overboard accidents tend to occur.

Quick Stop method

In an article in the NWSA newsletter, Sheila McCurdy Brown listed the ten points for overboard recovery—bearing in mind that "an incident might not follow the script."

1.   When a crewmember goes in the water, throw flotation and shout, "Crew overboard!"

2.   Designate a spotter who points and never takes her eyes off the victim.

3.   Bring the boat up into the wind and trim the mainsail close-hauled.

4.   Tack, keeping jib aback, and immediately run downwind with sails still trimmed in.

5.   Drop or furl the jib, if possible.

6.   When victim is abaft abeam, jibe.

7.   Sail up to the victim, slowing the boat as if to pick up a mooring.

8.   Stop alongside the victim.

9.   Toss a floating heaving line to the victim.

10.   Haul victim to boat and pull aboard.

In the summer of 1996, Sheila was racing the Newport-to-Bermuda Race—a biennial ocean race that starts in Newport, Rhode Island, and finishes in Bermuda. A few hours from the finish line—on a warm, clear, moonless night—with their spinnaker flying, a crewmember shouted, "Man overboard!" Sheila's brother, also a very experienced sailor, had gone overboard. But Sheila couldn't see anything forward of the mast and didn't know which side of the boat to look for her brother. While others searched the waves alongside, Sheila spun the helm and plastered the spinnaker against the rig, bringing the boat into the wind and to a dead stop. Hearing was difficult with a flogging main and flailing spinnaker, but there was still no sign of her brother. Then she called out, and he answered back from the foredeck. Like most prudent ocean racers and long-distance

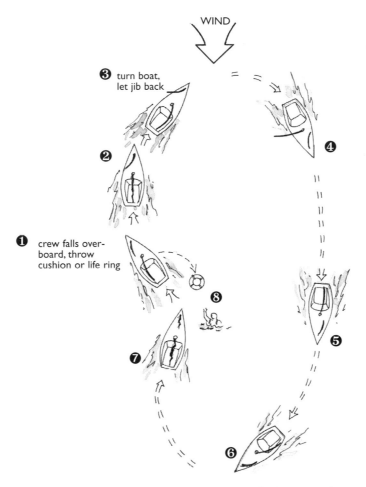

WIND

❸ turn boat,
let jib back

❷

❹

❶ crew falls over-
board, throw
cushion or life ring

❽

❺

❼

❻

Crew-overboard recovery with the Quick Stop method. As soon as the person falls in the water, throw a cushion or life ring to her (1). Immediately start turning the boat (2), allowing the jib to back to force your bow over, and continue turning downwind (3 and 4). Don't ease the main unless it keeps you from turning. Allow the boat to jibe so the sails are on proper side (5), then keep steering upwind toward close-hauled (6, 7). When downwind of victim (8), turn directly into the wind and stop alongside to pull her aboard.

cruisers, he had clipped his safety harness onto the jackline long before the bow lurched and threw him off balance. He was still attached to the boat, though not visible until the boat stopped dragging him through the water. Sheila estimates the whole episode took less than 30 seconds.

The lesson in all this, as Sheila points out, is that she was so familiar with overboard recovery procedures, she didn't have to think about what to do. Stopping the boat quickly kept her brother from being towed under the surface. She also notes that more than a couple of people were required to haul her brother aboard, and she recommends the LifeSling if you are sailing shorthanded.

Her brother also was wearing an inflatable PFD on his harness as a backup. If he had been separated from the boat, the flotation would have: held him higher in the water; made him a bigger, brighter target for the crew to see; and helped him to breathe more easily. As experienced as Sheila and her family are, she says they always practice overboard recovery before cruising to Maine each summer.

• •

"I was amazed at how much confidence I gained doing crew-overboard drills in three- to five-foot seas off Miami. I just pictured the drill in my mind, and every time we did it, we beat our previous time."

—Carol Ward, age 45

• •

The Quick Stop method does present some difficulties on small daysailers, particularly on highly responsive boats with such quick forward momentum that an immediate tack from a close-hauled course can take the boat too far upwind of the victim. In this case, a jibe is better and faster. On smaller boats that easily capsize, a quick tack will probably put any crew left aboard in the water too. If that's the case, allow the boat to round up into the wind and drift down on the person in the water.

Chapter 6

PREPARING YOURSELF AND THE BOAT

COLGATE 26

When women get together to talk about sailing goals, the conversation often turns to their desire to be prepared for any reasonable eventuality. Women express more "what if" concerns than men do, and we take the time to prepare ourselves and others for new experiences. Satisfying this concern allows us an enviable level of self-confidence, competence, and control.

I see a parallel in my own experience with snow skiing. I started to learn in earnest three years ago, at age 54. It was the first time I'd been on a slope in twenty-six years. My husband Steve hadn't skied in years and was very rusty—but he went straight up the quad chairlift, to the intermediate slopes. I took a lesson. And whenever I have the chance to continue the learning experience, I seek out a woman instructor and advance a little further. She tells me how well I'm doing, how good I look, corrects my mistakes gently, and senses when to challenge me. I don't ski fast, but I'm in control.

How does this relate to sailing? Your level of sailing enjoyment will rise in direct proportion to how well you prepare for the challenge and meet your personal needs.

"The only thing I could think about that first day was, will I be seasick? But all I had to do was take the helm and see what the boat could do, and I felt great!"

—Carol Ward, age 45

"My 'must-haves' when I go sailing are decent rain gear, comfortable quick-drying clothes, sailing gloves, and a hat."

—Betsy Alison, age 37

Part of that preparation is having the right safety equipment aboard and knowing how to use it, knowing some basic safety procedures, knowing how to communicate with other boats, and bringing the right gear aboard to protect yourself from the elements. In this chapter, you'll also learn about handling lines and knots.

CLOTHING FOR COMFORTABLE SAILING

There's an art to being comfortable on a boat and knowing what to bring for different types of sailing. When you take lessons, race, or practice in a small boat, you are much more active than when casually daysailing or cruising: you do more maneuvers, pull on more lines, and move about more often. Chances are, you'll also take some spray, so dress accordingly. Here's a list of items you should have in your sailing kit.

Sailing gloves

- **Sailing gloves.** Sailing gloves are sized extra small through extra large. They are made out of leather or a soft synthetic material, with padded palms, fingers cut off just above the middle joint for dexterity, a quick-drying synthetic back, and velcro closure. You can get women's gloves with full fingers to protect your nails, but they make handling deck hardware more cumbersome. For cold weather, use insulated full-fingered sailing gloves. Since all sailing gloves I know of are unisex, try a size smaller than your normal glove size.

- **Nonskid boat shoes.** These are a must. Sperry TopSider and Sebago are two popular brands found in most shoe stores, along with a variety of knock-offs. Harken makes an excellent, high-tech shoe found at most marine clothiers. You can choose leather moccasins, canvas sneakers, or athletic shoes—but make sure they have tightly grooved soles designed specifically to keep you from slipping on salty or wet decks. To check, bend the soles to open up the grooves. You should see many grooves, with channels to direct water out. If the grooves are spread wide and are open, or the sole is bumpy (like a tennis shoe), the shoe won't

Boat shoes

give you good footing. Avoid black soles that can leave marks on decks. Protect your toes: avoid sandals, even if they have "boat-shoe" bottoms.

In northern climes, you need a pair of rubber or neoprene sailing boots with nonskid bottoms. They come in low- and high-cut models, laced or unlaced, and are typically sold in marine supply stores.

● **A hat that stays on.** Big floppy straw hats aren't practical. A low-profile cap with a good beak stays on better, and a strap that clips from the back of the hat to your shirt or jacket keeps your hat attached to you. If you can't find a hat strap, tie a piece of light line through something on the hat and a buttonhole on your shirt, or a bathing suit strap. For those who want more protection, there are special hats with lightweight flaps to cover your ears and neck, which are popular among recreational fishermen. The Ultimate hat costs a little more and isn't elegant, but it floats, has a built-in strap, brim all around, quick-drying fabric, and grommet holes to keep your head cool. Some women like visors, but they don't protect your scalp or dyed hair from the sun's rays.

● **Sunglasses.** Get the best UV protection you can afford. All-plastic glasses (including lenses) help you avoid injury, if you're hit while wearing them. A flexible frame is a bonus if you're prone to putting your glasses down where someone can sit or step on them. Polarized lenses help you see contours and underwater obstructions better. Be sure to buy a strap to keep them from going overboard. If you wear contacts, you'll definitely want sunglasses to keep spray (especially salt spray) out of your eyes. I wore Serengetti H2Optix glasses during the photo shoot for this book, done in glaring sunlight. Lightweight, with a floating strap, I found them very comfortable and effective.

Woman-sized foul-weather gear

● **Foul-weather gear.** It has an ominous name, but if you take sailing lessons in northern regions or sail where it's cool, a water-resistant windbreaker just won't cut it. Foul-weather gear is specifically designed for sailors with features you won't find in other clothes. Among these are heat-sealed, stitched, and waterproof tape-covered seams on the inside; hand-warmer pockets; tight inside cuffs to keep water from leaking past ankles and wrists; covered, rust-proof zippers; reflective tape on the hide-away hood and sleeves; durable cloth on the seat and knees; and a high-bib pant to keep water out when you're hit by a wave. Many fabrics are labeled breathable, but they can be very different in quality and use.

Helly Hansen has made a serious commitment to women sailors with a full line of sailing clothes, including foul weather gear. Douglas Gill makes suits specifically for women in two grades (lighter weight and oceangoing), sized 6 to 16.

One of the best sailing shop and catalog outfits around is Team One Newport, owned by wiry but petite Martha MacKechnie, a world-class small-boat sailor and ocean racer. An expert on what fits, she says that whether male or female, we're all built completely differently. "A women needs to find a product line that fits her body type." Martha finds that Patagonia and Henri-Lloyd tend to run long and a little bigger; Musto is shorter and a little stockier with a medium broad bib size; and Gill is pretty average. Martha advises, "Don't look for just women's sizes; look for what will work for you."

A good suit can run at least $300, and lesser models can be found for under $100. I recommend investing smart the first time out. The cheaper versions eventually rip or leak. The good stuff will last for years.

- **Warm-weather apparel.** Martha suggests a shirt for sun protection (like the shirts produced by Railriders, made in women's sizes) and quick-dry shorts. I prefer to wear cotton because its cool, but cotton does have drawbacks. When it's wet, it gets heavy, doesn't dry as quickly as synthetics (which are not as cool), and becomes stiff if doused in salt water. I like to wear loose-fitting shorts, a tank top, long- or short-sleeved tees, and a comfortable bathing suit underneath. Some women like stretch knit shorts and athletic tops. Bring a long-sleeved shirt to avoid sunburn, and socks to protect the tops of your feet. If you do wear a bathing suit, consider a two-piece suit over a one-piece suit, for ease in going to the bathroom.

- **Cold-weather apparel.** Cold, wet, and uncomfortable just doesn't mix with sailing pleasure. Martha recommends a good layering system with products that

"**W**hen I'm sailing in cool weather, there's nothing like wicking layers—polypropylene fleece-over-silk long johns under leggings."

—Stephanie Argyris, age 47

wick or don't hold moisture. For the first layer against your skin, she says Patagonia Capilene underwear is fabulous. With an antibacterial treatment that wards off body odors, it comes in five different weights in women's sizes. For the second layer, she uses any type of polypropylene fleece because it's warm, comfortable, and lightweight. Companies like Patagonia, High Seas,

Polar fleece vest and long-sleeved polar fleece pullover.

Woolrich, and Columbia all use it for sailing apparel. Martha wears Patagonia's Expedition top and bottom, and they're sized for women!

Blue jeans are not good on a boat. When they get wet they get heavy, and as they dry they feel and act like cardboard. Itchy wool is much heavier than fleece and stays cold and soggy when wet. Skiers and sailors discovered fleece at about the same time—for jacket linings, layering pieces like vests, pants, long-sleeve tops, socks, and hats. I use some of the same clothes for skiing as I do for sailing in cold waters.

● **Sunblock, lip balm, face cream.** In the latest controversy, higher number protection sunblocks like 36 and 42 might be no better than 18. Regardless, pick the one that works best for you and apply it often in hot or cold weather. Don't be fooled by a cloudy day. UV rays still get through. Avoid greasy gels and lotions that stain clothing: they'll do the same to the deck. For ultimate protection, one of the best sunblocks is zinc oxide. This has always come in a messy white or colored cream, but it's now available in a clear gel.

Don't forget lip balms. There are several on the market with UV protection and should be worn at all times. Ordinary lipstick is okay, but not as effective. After sailing—particularly if your sunblock wore off or you forgot it altogether—use repeated applications of an aloe gel, and later on, fragrance-free lotions with aloe. These not only heal and soften, but they work well as face moisturizers and makeup removers. Why fragrance-free? Odors seem to attract no-see-ums in warm climates—which is not particularly fun when you're enjoying the sunset after a nice day of sailing.

SEASICK REMEDIES

There are plenty of remedies to bring along and smart ways to keep seasickness at bay. I like acupressure wrist bands (developed for morning sickness). Some women prefer a mild potion, like organic ginger. In extreme conditions, there are over-the-counter motion sickness drugs, such as Bonine and Dramamine; these, however, can make you drowsy. Prescription drugs like the Scopolamine patch work well, but this can produce a dry-mouth feeling and disorientation. One patch is supposed to last a week. Never cut it in half, thinking you'll simply get a smaller dosage. Any that seeps out just gives you a huge dose all at once.

To lower your chances of getting seasick, stay above deck in fresh air in rough weather, breathe deeply, relax, watch the horizon, get on the helm, and make sure you eat.

"Lord Byron used to get seasick every time he hit a storm . . . I'm in good company!"

—Fern Zabriskie, age "27–33–44: pick one, I don't normally tell the truth!"

Here are some more tips:

- Carry a small, waterproof duffel for all your gear, wallet, and keys. Leave your handbag at home.

- If you wear makeup foundation, mascara, eyeliner, etc., they should be waterproof.

- To avoid tangles in long hair, comb a conditioner through it, then braid it or pull it back. You'll also avoid catching your hair in fittings on the boat.

- There's not much you can do for your nails, except keep them short. They're bound to break, and nail polish will rub off as you handle lines. Use a lot of hand cream on cuticles to keep them soft.

- If you bring a camera, make sure it's waterproof.

- Wear minimal jewelry. Small studs in your ears are alright. So is a waterproof watch with strong watch band. But take off rings, loose bracelets, and loop or dangling earrings. If these catch on something, you could get hurt. And you won't be a happy camper if you lose a stone.

DIET AND SAILING

Women today are bombarded with advice about diet and nutrition—whether we sail or not. Still, there are some do's and don'ts that apply specifically to sailors.

- Drinking more than one glass of wine the night before a sail isn't a good idea. Minor hangovers can be greatly exacerbated by choppy conditions on the water. Big hangovers get in the way of quick responses when needed.

- Avoid fatty or greasy foods and too much caffeine. You don't want to be jittery, and anything that might unsettle your stomach can turn a beautiful day on the water into an unpleasant experience.

- A low-fat, high-carbohydrate, high-protein diet is good.

- Always eat and drink plenty of water before you sail. An empty stomach and dehydration encourage seasickness.

- In hot weather, drink plenty of water while sailing. Freeze a bottle of water the night before and you'll have refreshing, cold water all day.

- Sugary sodas don't sit as well as plain water or Gatorade.

- When it's time for a snack, stick to bland, wholesome foods like peanut butter or plain crackers and an apple. They're easy to digest, won't cause discomfort if it gets rough, and are recommended for tough passages when you might not feel like eating.

- If you've been told to bring lunch, cheese sandwiches, carrot sticks, and apples are always easy to handle. When I cooked on ocean races, peanut butter and jelly sandwiches were always popular!

LIFESAVING EQUIPMENT

Many sailors think that if they're in waters near home and only out for a few hours, nothing can happen. So why worry? But there are rules that apply to all boats, regardless of size or where they sail. You'll learn about lifesaving equipment in the following section. Go to a marine supply store—such as BOAT/U.S. or West Marine—and you can find a myriad of safety equipment for both you and your boat.

Life vests

The Coast Guard requires you to have a Coast Guard–approved PFD (personal flotation device) for every person aboard. The designation *Coast Guard–approved* relates to amount of buoyancy, and it only applies to vests made in the United States.

Life vests are PFDs, and they come in a range of sizes, shapes, and degrees of efficiency, from Type I to V. At Offshore Sailing School, we use Type III vests, which are Coast Guard–approved and relatively comfortable, with flotation back and front.

1. Type II life vest; **2.** Type III life vest; **3.** Type V life vest.

Some schools use Type II vests, which are less comfortable, less expensive, quite bulky around your neck, and tend to stick out over your bust. The Type V PFD, which recently gained Coast Guard approval, is a small harness or fanny pack that inflates when you hit the water—either automatically or by pulling a string. It's by far the most comfortable (although relatively expensive), and it packs away nicely in a duffel when not in use. Unfortunately, only vests worn by water skiers are made for the contours of a woman's figure, but these are not Coast Guard–approved.

Life vests should be worn on deck at all times. But in very light air on hot days, anything other than the inflatable type can be pretty uncomfortable. Use common sense. Consider buying your own vest—one that really fits you well—rather than relying on what you'll find aboard a friend's boat. For further safety, many sailors attach to their vests: a small strobe light that flashes and attracts attention when you're in the water; a whistle to blow (instead of trying to yell) if help is near enough to hear.

A float coat is a waterproof jacket for sailing in cold waters that has a lining made out of the same materials used on a life vest. Although bulky, it will keep you warm and safely afloat should you fall in the water.

Other safety equipment

Your boat should have lifelines to keep the crew from slipping over the side. Check them periodically for wear and tear. The point where the plastic-coated wire runs through the stanchions is one vulnerable place.

SAILING IN COLD WATERS

In cold water areas, where even a short dip can lower your body temperature to risky levels, hypothermia becomes a true concern.

On one of our graduate cruises in the San Juan Islands near Seattle, a show-off jumped into the water with great bravado when we anchored for lunch. Within seconds, he turned bright pink. After about a minute, we were helping him climb back up the ladder and go below, where we covered his shaking body with mounds of blankets. When we cruised in Maine, another man did the same, jumping into the too-cold water. What's the point of putting yourself at risk when you know hypothermia's a possibility? Fortunately, neither man had reached hypothermic levels, which can be fatal if not treated properly.

According to the Coast Guard, hypothermia is subnormal temperature in the central nervous system—the heart and brain. Survival time is affected by how much body fat you have, how much you exert yourself (as little as possible is best), and whether your head is in or out of the water. That's why good life vests are so important. The vest will not only keep your head up and out of the water; it will also keep you warm. Since body heat dissipates faster in water than in air, you want to get out of the water as quickly as possible. If you must wait, try to assume a fetal position by hugging your knees close to your chest. If you've capsized, stay with the boat and don't try to swim away. Distances are much farther than you think, and rescuers will spot your overturned boat before they see you. Here's what the Coast Guard recommends for helping someone with hypothermia:

1. Move the person to shelter and warmth as rapidly as possible.
2. Gently remove all wet clothing.
3. Apply heat to the head, neck, sides, and groin with hot moist towels (about 105 degrees) or hot water bottles and electric blankets, if available. One or two rescuers can also remove all their clothing and use their body heat to warm the victim by lying alongside her naked body, using a sleeping bag or blanket to conserve body heat.
4. Don't give the victim anything to drink (especially avoid alcohol).
5. Don't wrap the person in a blanket without another source of heat, unless the blanket is being used to protect against further heat loss before treatment.

A throwable life cushion is required for small, open-cockpit boats. These life cushions– considered a Type IV PFD–*do not meet* Coast Guard regulations for having life vests aboard; but they do qualify as a throwable device for overboard recovery.

Your boat should carry at least one anchor, with a length of anchor rode that is sufficient for the area and water depth you sail in. You should also have oars or paddles.

On cruising boats, you'll need at least one fire extinguisher in case of fire. Life rings, LifeSling, or similar crew-overboard recovery device (the use of the LifeSling is covered in chapter 5) should be included with any boat where it isn't *easy to* climb on board from the water unassisted. Handheld and aerial flares appropriate for where you'll be sailing (check USCG regulations for the minimum, SOLAS for what should be carried) allow you to call attention to your boat from far away with a bright explosion of light or bright orange smoke. All crew members or at least the boat should be equipped with a strobe light that intermittently flashes a bright white light. If you get into trouble you can transmit a signal to pinpoint your boat's position using a 406 MHz EPIRB (emergency position-indicating radio beacon); it's far superior to the old 121.5 MHz units. It is also always a good idea to carry a handheld, waterproof VHF radio in case of emergency. An emergency can occur anytime, so it's prudent to carry a quality life raft adequate for the maximum number of people you might have aboard. To check on this or other emergency equipment check out the specialty web site at <*http://www.equiped.org*>.

COMMUNICATING WITH OTHER BOATS AND WITH SHORE

VHF (which stands for very high frequency) radiotelephones are typically found on larger boats, but we keep them on the Colgate 26 for safety purposes. VHFs either come in hand held models or are wired into a boat's electrical system.

Marine radiotelephones are used mainly to contact other boats and for emergencies. If you have a VHF aboard, keep it set to Channel 16. This channel is used for emergencies or to make initial contact with another party.

Women sometimes develop radiotelephone phobia, which is unfounded and easily overcome. There is a certain etiquette to using a radiotelephone. After making initial contact on Channel 16, switch to another channel right away. The following scenario is the proper way to hail another boat. While holding in the button on the mouthpiece, call the name of the boat you're trying to reach, and then identify your boat. "*Sundance*, this is *Moon River*. Over." The response will probably be, "This is *Moon River*, go ahead *Sundance*." You reply, "This is *Sundance*, switching to Channel 68. Over." (You select the channel to switch to.) When the switch is made, repeat the initial call. When the other boat responds, proceed with a quick conversation. It's appropriate to say "Over" at the end of each transmission to indicate it's okay for the other person to speak, although I don't hear this as often as I used to. Technically, you are also supposed to use a call sign in addition to the boat's name, but I don't hear that, either. When you're completely finished, the initial caller says, "This is *Sundance*. Out." The party called acknowledges, ending with "Out."

Keep conversations to a minimum, never use swear words, and tell kids this radio is not a telephone. Don't ever call SOS or Mayday unless you're truly in danger to life and limb—never because you're out of wind, or need a tow, or in a situation that isn't life threatening.

Radiotelephones operate in a line-of-sight range, with an antenna on your stern or at the top of your mast. A tall hill or mountain can obstruct this signal.

If you don't have a cell phone aboard, or you're out of range and need to talk to someone ashore, you can reach a marine operator through your VHF. If you have trouble making contact because of static, lower the squelch button and try again.

Although a VHF is technically only for boat-to-boat communication, in some areas sailors use their VHF to contact marinas for slip reservations, to make reservations for repairs, meals, etc.

ELECTRICAL HAZARDS

One of the joys of small boat sailing is being able to cartop or trailer your boat just about anywhere and enjoy rivers, lakes, and coastlines. However, some launch areas are bordered by low electrical wires. These won't affect powerboats, but they are a great danger to sailboats.

If you trailer or cartop your boat, you'll be rigging your mast when you get to the launch area. Before you set the mast up on your boat and slide your boat into the water, look up and check for overhead wires. Masts and electrical lines don't marry well, and every year you hear of someone who was electrocuted while launching a boat. While this is rare, it's something to be aware of.

WHEN A SHROUD OR STAY BREAKS

Not much can go wrong mechanically on a small, open-cockpit boat. But parts of the boat can loosen up or break with little or no notice. The shrouds and stays keep your mast upright, and they are under a lot of pressure when your sails are set. If one snaps, the mast might break or go over the side. But if you know the right procedure, you have a good chance of saving your rig.

If a shroud breaks while you're sailing, try to tack quickly to put the pressure on the good shroud. If you have a spinnaker halyard, you can use it to replace the broken shroud. Since the halyard is usually double ended, cleat one end to the mast. Leave enough slack in the line so you can tie (or hook) the other end into a toerail or stanchion base near to where the broken shroud was fastened. Tighten up on the cleated end of the halyard, then get your sails down or sail into a protected area.

If no other boats are around to hail for a tow and you don't have a radiotelephone, hopefully you brought your cell phone along and you're close enough to land to get a signal. If you didn't, don't panic. Assess your situation. If you're close enough to shore, paddle home. If shore is too far away, anchor. If you're in deep water and don't have enough anchor rode, paddle towards shore and shallower water. Chances are you weren't very far off when the problem occurred (especially in a small, open-cockpit boat), and someone will pass close by to help out.

While you're waiting, you can get very creative and figure out how you might tie off a sail to catch the wind or *scull* the boat towards shore by moving your tiller (and the rudder below) back and forth in long sweeps.

As you do more sailing, you'll see how aware you become of other sailboats and how sensitive sailors are to each other's well-being. I have, more than once, changed my course to go over to another boat that looks like it might be in need of assistance.

> "Learning to tie knots just takes a
> little patience and persistence."
>
> —Holly O'Hare, age 29

KNOTS AND LINE HANDLING

Ropes and lines are important tools for a sailor. They help you harness the power of the wind in your sails, secure your boat to a dock or a mooring, and help you handle heavy items like your anchor. Without lines, sailors would be lost—and once you start sailing, you'll understand why lines are so invaluable onboard.

Knowing how to tie several basic knots will make sailing easier for you—and safer. It's also important to know how to put a line on a cleat or around a piling and how to properly throw a line to someone ashore. Coiling and organizing line is also a vital skill. Otherwise, you would be swimming a sea of confused spaghetti onboard, which will impede your sailing and can also be dangerous.

Learning about knots can be confusing at first, as I described in the first stanza of "How Not to Tie a Knot," a poem I wrote after my first sailing lesson.

> *The nautical knot, a confusing lot*
> *Of rope entwined around, about*
> *A complex slot*
> *Of ins and outs*
> *Oh, dear—how not to tie a knot!*

Today I can't imagine it was that confusing—though as a lefty, I tie some knots and coil lines opposite to the way instructors tried to teach me. It really doesn't matter how you tie the knot, as long as it comes out correctly.

Knots you'll use onboard

In this section, you'll learn to tie several basic knots that can be used in many places aboard. You might want to practice these as your read along, so get yourself a 3-foot length of line.

The bowline

The bowline is one of the most commonly used knots because it doesn't slip or jam and is very easy to untie. It was used in the old days on square sails to hold the tack forward toward the bow. To practice this knot, find a rail, post, or something on your boat to loop one end of the rope around. The longer end of the line would normally be cleated or tied off. That's the *standing* part of the line.

Many instructors use the rabbit-and-hole story to teach this knot: "The rabbit comes out of the hole, goes around the tree, and back down the hole." Make a small loop (the hole) in the standing part of the line and hold it in one hand. Make sure the top part of the loop runs counterclockwise over the loop. Then, with the other hand, bring the free end (the rabbit) up through the loop (1 in illustration), around the back of the standing part of the line (the tree) from right to left (2 in illustration), and back down through the loop (the hole; 3 in illustration), and pull tight. You can use a post or chair leg to practice this knot.

It might take you a few tries to get it right. Here's how I felt about the bowline in the poem I referred to above:

> *Hand over hand, under one*
> *A twist and over, almost done*
> *Now pull it through and back the same*
> *Good grief! Let's start from scratch again!*

And here's how I imagine my instructor felt, when he showed our group how to do it:

> *One is the standing end, okay?*
> *Loose end over, that's the way*
> *Twist the left as right flips under*
> *You've nearly got it now, by thunder!*
> *Around the standing, through the loop—*
> *My word, how did I get this group?*

Among other uses, a bowline is used to tie sheets into the clew of a sail, make a loop to hook around a piling, and tie two lines together into one long line. To untie a bowline, no matter how much tension has been on the knot, just bend or work the knot a little, and the loops will loosen enough for you to take it apart easily.

The stop knot

Bowline

The stop knot is used on the ends of lines that are run through blocks, such as jibsheets and mainsheets, so the sheet won't slip completely through the block and fly out of reach. For example, when you fall off and head downwind, you let the mainsheet run as you push the sail all the way out. Without a stop knot, the free end of the mainsheet might slip out of the block and end up way out over the water. Place a stop knot in the ends of sheets to avoid losing them.

To make a stop knot, begin at the free end of the line, make two loops in any one direction, run the free end back through the loops, and pull tight. The knot won't come out until you pull the two loops apart.

Another place to use this knot is at ends of halyards, to keep them from sliding all the way to the top of the mast. But don't put stop knots in the ends of spinnaker sheets and guys; when it

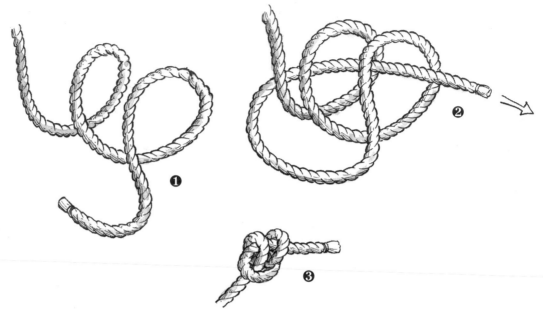

Stop knot. Recommended in place of figure eight to keep end of a jibsheet, mainsheet, or halyard from running through their blocks. **1.** Make two loops in any direction. **2.** Run the free (loose) end back through both loops. **3.** Pull tight.

comes time to get that big balloon sail down, you want the sheets to run free to allow the sail to collapse. If the sheets stop in the blocks, the chute might fly high in the air, way out over the water and too high to grasp and pull in easily.

The figure eight

The figure eight can also be used at the ends of sheets and ropes, but I prefer the stop knot because a figure eight can loosen on its own. To tie a figure eight properly, make a loop with the free end first, passing under the standing part of the rope (1), then over it and back through the top loop, from back to front (2). The end result is that the free end comes out on the inside and over the first loop (3). It doesn't matter if you do this right- or left-handed. Just make that first loop in whichever hand is comfortable.

Figure-eight knot.

The square knot

The square knot is most commonly used to tie down a reefed or furled sail. If it's tied incorrectly, it becomes a granny knot, which can be impossible to untie. Have you ever put an extra knot on your running shoes to keep the original bow from coming loose? If you tied a granny knot, chances are you had to pull off your shoe without loosening the knot at the end of your run.

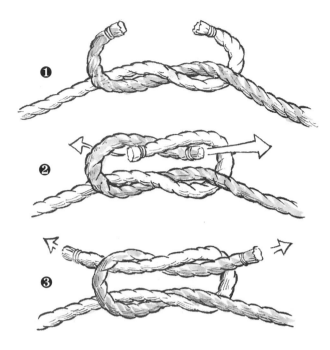

Square knot.

To tie a square knot, pass the line around your sail, for example, holding both free ends, one in each hand. Loop one end over the other end (1). If you are right-handed, pass the left end under the right end, then the right end over the left (2). (If you are left-handed, pass the right end under the left end, the left end over the right.) This results in the lines coming out of the loop side by side— on one side, over the loop; on the other side, under the loop (3). When you pull tight, the line will stay firmly in place, but it is easily untied by pushing the two sides against each other.

The half-hitch

The half-hitch, commonly used to secure a line to a post, is very easy to tie, adjust, and untie. Whether you are left- or right-handed, the effect is the same. Pass the free end of the rope around the post from behind and toward you (1). Pass the free end under the standing end, then back over the standing end and through the loop you just made (2). Now you have a half-hitch. But to keep the hitch from slipping, you really need two half-hitches. Make another identical loop under the first half-hitch, and pull tight (3). Although the standing end (the end that would be attached to a cleat, for example) is led straight through the two loops, it won't slip because the two hitches are pulling against it. But this knot isn't fool-proof. If the line goes slack, which takes tension off the line it's hanging from, the loops could eventually loosen.

Two half-hitches.

Clove hitch. A good knot for tying fenders to lifelines and securing a rope around a post. 1. Run free end of line around lifeline and back over itself twice. 2. Feed free end under the second loop on the lifeline. 3. Both ends of line are side by side under loop, pointing in opposite direction. Pull tight.

The clove hitch

The clove hitch is held in place by friction and used to secure fenders to lifelines or stanchions. It is also a quick way to fasten a rope around a post.

Start by running the free end of the line around the lifeline or post, and back over itself, making a full loop or turn. Then run the line back around the lifeline or post again, and feed the line up under itself (that second loop or turn). Both ends of the line should be lying snugly next to each other under the second loop, but pointing in opposite directions. When you tighten the hitch, the rope stays in place. For added security, tie a few half-hitches along the standing end.

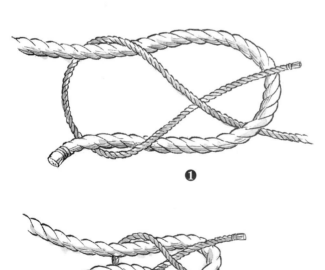

Sheet bend.

The sheet bend

The sheet bend comes in handy when you need to tie two ropes of different sizes together. Imagine you've run aground and need help getting off. A friend comes along in a powerboat, but neither of you has a long-enough line. Together, though, you can come up with enough length using two different sized ropes.

Make a loop in the larger line and hold the two sides of the line alongside each other (but don't cross one over the other). Take the smaller-diameter line and pass the short end under and out through the top of the loop and back under the two side-by-side ends of the larger line (1). Then run the smaller line back under itself and pull tight (2). This knot also works well when you need to rig a springline using two short lines of different diameter.

Coiling a line

You should coil lines so they're available to use at all times. Coiling lines will also keep your boat shipshape. If you throw your docklines into a heap in a locker, the next time you need them you'll spend a lot of time trying to find the ends and undo the knots! So before you put any lines away, coil them.

Except for anchor lines, most rope used aboard boats today is braided. Braided line won't tend to kink badly if it's coiled in the wrong direction. But anchor line is often three-strand line and twisted in one direction when it's made. So if you coil it against the twist, which happens to left-handed people like me, you can end up with a tangled mess. To coil a line, hold in your right hand the end of the line you want to handle last the next time you use that line. Then, make a series of clockwise loops with your left hand, twisting the line slightly as you go so it hangs straight. Grab each of the loops at the top in your right hand as you make them. You start your coil with the end you want to use *last* because when you're finished coiling, the end you want to use *first* will be on top and ready to go.

The size of the loops you make depends on the thickness and length of the line. Large docklines, which are harder to hold when all the loops are made, should be coiled in fairly large (2 feet or larger) loops. Smaller lines, like a jibsheet, don't require such big loops.

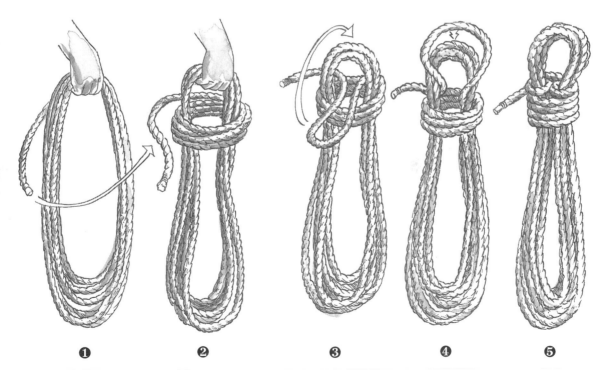

❶   ❷   ❸   ❹   ❺

Coiling a line. Start with end you want to use last next time. **1.** Make a series of clockwise loops and hold these at the top. **2.** Wrap end of line tightly several times around top third of coils below your hand. **3.** Make loop in free end. **4.** Pass the loop through coils above the wraps and down over top. **5.** Pull free end tight.

Chapter 7

SMART SAILING

"**W**e had thirty-five to forty knots in the Spring Series out of Rye Yacht Club in New York. I wasn't afraid and did what I had to do. It all came together then."

—Kim Auburn, age 39

As you sail more and more, you'll gain knowledge and sail more intelligently. This chapter on "Smart Sailing" covers the areas where your learning curve will continually climb: on achieving the right sail shapes for speed and performance, on understanding the weather around you, and on getting the most out of the wind. True sailors are sailors for a lifetime: they never stop learning. Now that you've mastered some of the basics, these are the areas where you can fine-tune your skills.

WHY SAIL SHAPE IS IMPORTANT

The more you sail, the more you notice a difference between sailors with knowledge and pride and those who don't know what they're doing or don't care. The way sails look affects the way the boat sails.

Think of sails as wings of a plane. Air passing over and under the wings creates *lift*, which eventually gets the plane off the ground. *Airflow* affects sails in much the same way. As long as the flow is smooth on both sides of the sail, it produces lift that pulls the sail in a sideways and forward direction. When air stops flowing smoothly over one side or the other, the boat slows down. You can "see" airflow by reading the telltales on your sail, as we did in Chapter 5.

Sometimes you'll see a jib or mainsail with scallops or wrinkles along the luff. These scallops are usually cured by tightening the halyard. If the sail is attached to the forestay or mast with toggles, scallops appear when the halyard is too loose. If the sail has a boltrope that goes up in a groove, there will be wrinkles. You want a tight, smooth luff. Wrinkles or scallops disrupt the airflow over that area of the sail and cause its efficiency to drop dramatically.

If you've done everything you can to get your scallops or wrinkles out (the halyard is up as high as it can go; downhauls or cunninghams are tightened), consider two other factors. Sails constantly stretch as wind strength increases, and they might eventually *blow out*, meaning they are no longer able to keep their shape. Or the cut of the sail might be wrong for the length of your forestay; this is obvious if your halyard is up as far as it will go and the luff still isn't smooth. An old sail can sometimes be recut. But it's usually less costly in the long run to buy a new sail that's tailor-made for your boat.

Sailmakers build *draft* into a sail. This extra material allows the sail to curve and determines how full or flat you can make your sail. Why should you care whether a sail is flat or full? In specific wind and wave conditions, the sail's shape makes a huge difference in the comfort and speed of the boat.

Think of sail shape as gears on a racing car. Full sails are low gear and flat sails are high gear. In flat seas, where you encounter the least resistance from waves, you want flat sails (high gear) for maximum speed. When seas are lumpy, the boat slows down every time it hits a wave and needs help to accelerate. So you want the sails that are fuller (low gear). In higher winds, when the boat is going flat out and not affected by wave action, the sails should be flat. In light air, as the boat slows down, shift to low gear and make the sails fuller. Racing sailors constantly change sail shape to maintain or increase their speed. In everyday sailing, shape is important for comfort.

You also want air to exit smoothly off the leech—particularly from the jib to the backside of the mainsail, where undisturbed airflow creates lift for faster, more efficient sailing.

THE SHAPE OF SPEED

Suppose you're sailing close-hauled and the wind starts to shift aft a little, which means the wind has now moved from coming over the forward part of the boat to coming over the side of the boat. You want to stay on the same course, so you ease your sails. Remember to use your hand as a brake to adjust the jibsheet. If the wind shift is slight, let the jib out a tiny bit at a time and watch the telltales until they stream aft. If the wind shifts back ahead, take the sail in a few cranks at a time until your telltales are streaming again.

New sailors sometimes turn the winch handle madly without looking up—and the sail ends up flat against the spreaders! As you trim, watch the helmsman, listen to others, read the wind or the boat's direction, and look at the sail and the telltales.

The same movements apply to trimming the mainsail, unless you're making big course changes—from a close-hauled course to a broad reach, or from a broad reach to a run. In those cases, you might have to let the sail out quickly to avoid excessive heeling and to make it easier for the driver to bear away. When the boat heels drastically because the sails haven't been eased, the rudder lifts out of the water and stalls. This makes it almost impossible to turn away from the wind.

Mainsail shape and controls

A mainsail usually has draft built near the middle of the sail, and its shape is adjusted with the outhaul, cunningham, halyard tension, backstay tension, the traveler, boom vang, and mainsheet.

When you're sailing to windward, the draft should be forward. To achieve this, tighten up on the cunningham. The sail should also be as close to the centerline of the boat as possible. Sometimes, this means you have the traveler car (where the outboard end of the mainsheet attaches to the traveler) past centerline and up to windward.

If you feel the boat is *overpowered* (heeling too much, too much tug on the tiller or wheel, see photo on page 85), ease the traveler first. You can keep easing the traveler to reduce heeling and control the boat better, but you might have to ease the mainsheet too. When you ease the mainsheet, this causes the boom to rise and frees the leech. As a result the top of the sail will *twist off* and spill air out. To cure this, tighten the boom vang to pull the boom down again (see illustration).

Sometimes you want to spill air in the top portion of the mainsail. This happens in heavy air, when the extra force at the top of the mast causes more heeling and less control. To open up the top of the sail when you're close-hauled, ease the mainsheet and the boom vang just enough to let the air spill out aloft.

Normally, you keep the mainsail flat when close-hauled by using the mainsheet. But in very light air, if you pull too tight on the mainsheet, the leech tightens and the sail loses its shape. To avoid this, keep the mainsheet just slightly tensioned and pull the traveler up to windward to keep the boom along the centerline of the boat.

The leech should be tight and smooth, but not cupped to windward.

Twist will occur at the top of the mainsail when mainsheet and boom vang are eased. Boat A's boom is horizontal to the boat, with both vang and mainsheet tight, and the sail is flat. The boom on Boat B lifts up when the vang and mainsheet are eased. This frees the leech and allows the top of the sail to curve forward. Tighten the boom vang to pull the boom down again.

When the leech is too tight, airflow bends in its cupped edge and flows off to windward. Since this flow is at the back end of the boat, its force pushes the stern of the boat to leeward (away from the wind). This creates too much weather helm and makes it hard to steer. The more the stern is pushed away from the wind, the more the bow wants to round up toward the wind. If you're steering, you'll feel a terrific tug on the tiller or wheel: the tiller or wheel will probably be over as far it can go, perpendicular to the water flow, and the boat won't respond.

To correct this, ease the boom vang and the mainsheet just enough to feel the boat straighten out. Or, if you have an adjustable backstay, tighten up on the backstay to bend the mast. This causes the mast to curve slightly, which brings the draft of the sail forward and loosens the leech.

The cunningham tensions the luff and moves the draft forward on the mainsail. Pull tight for a smooth luff upwind, and loosen it up for the best sail shape on a run. When sailing downwind, you not only ease off the cunningham completely to open up your entire sail area, but you sometimes ease the halyard down a little too. Both adjustments help increase the draft and move it aft. Of course, as you plan your turn to go back up wind, you want to put back all those tensioners.

Remember, when you ran the foot of the mainsail along the boom, you secured it at the outboard end with the outhaul. The other end of the outhaul leads through the boom to a cam cleat near the middle. When you tighten the outhaul, you stretch the

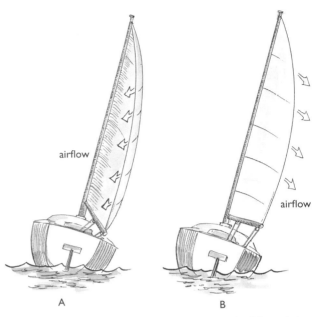

When there is too much **mainsheet tension**, the leech of the main is cupped to windward as in Boat A, causing airflow off the leech to port, forcing the boat to round up towards the wind. With proper mainsheet tension (Boat B), air flows aft off the leech.

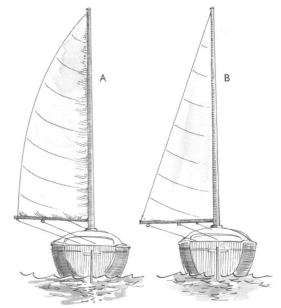

Fullness in the main is desirable when sailing downwind: Boat A shows what happens when you ease the outhaul—to loosen the foot—and also ease the halyard slightly to soften the luff. The result is that the leech curves, allowing the sail to bag and capture more wind. On Boat B the outhaul and halyard are tight and the sail is flat, which is a less effective sail shape on this point of sail.

foot of the sail; when you ease the outhaul, you bag the foot of the sail. The wrinkles that appear along the foot when the outhaul is eased out are not very pretty. But they are desirable when you're sailing on a run and you want fullness in the sail.

Women can be good sail trimmers: we are good at planning, we cope well with changing environments in our lives, and most of us are quite orderly. It's a piece of cake to remember all the things we just did to shape our sails.

Headsail shape and controls

Your jibs are your headsails, and they are designed to have maximum draft at about 35 percent from the leading edge for upwind sailing. The shape of these sails is primarily controlled by halyard, jibsheet, and backstay tension. Again, the luff and leech should be smooth and tight (but not too tight) when sailing close-hauled.

A sag along the luff, created by a loose halyard or backstay, deflects airflow where it's needed most. You might see sag on larger cruising boats, which is caused by the weight of heavy roller-furling genoas, or on a racing boat with an adjustable backstay. Not much can be done for the cruising boat, except to tighten the halyard as much as possible.

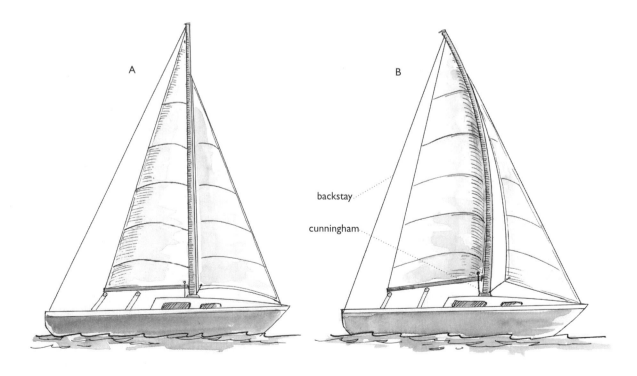

To keep draft from moving aft in heavy air as shown in Boat A, tighten the backstay and the cunningham on the main. This bends the mast aft, frees the leech, brings draft forward, and flattens your sails—usually desirable in heavy air and relatively flat seas.

When an adjustable backstay is tightened, the forestay is also tightened and the draft in the sail moves forward. The tighter the forestay, the flatter the sail. At some point the draft is too far forward, the sail is too flat, and efficiency is so greatly reduced that the backstay must be eased to make it easier to handle the boat and get back in the groove.

When you ease off the backstay downwind to take the bend out of the mast and open more mainsail area to the wind, you also soften the forestay. But downwind, your headsail will either become ineffective or you'll set a spinnaker (a big, colorful, balloon-shaped sail that flies out in front of the boat), and the forestay is no longer a factor.

Jibsheet tension controls the leech of a headsail. If the sail is sheeted in too hard, you see backwind on the mainsail. But when you're close-hauled, a little backwind is often desirable. If the sheets are eased out too far, the slot between the mainsail and the headsail opens up. Since airflow isn't forced through a constricted area, there's less pressure and less lift on the sails. The result is, the boat won't *point* as well (sail close to the wind).

Jibsheets are led through movable blocks, which are sometimes called cars, on tracks on either side of the boat. These tracks typically run from a point several feet forward of the mast and back along the deck to a point aft of the mast. Their length depends on the length of the foot of the headsail. The location of the track from the boat's centerline affects how well the boat sails. This is called the *jib lead angle*, and it will vary from boat to boat.

How to set up your headsails

When a headsail is set properly on the wind, telltales along the luff should break at the same time, from top to bottom. Whether they break in unison depends on where the jib leads are placed. If the lead is too far aft, the top of the sail starts to luff first. In this case, the foot of the sail is too tight and the leech is too loose. To correct this, move the jib lead forward a notch or two.

If the lead is too far forward, the lower part of the sail luffs first. The foot of the sail looks rounded or cupped, and the leech is too tight, which causes backwind in the mainsail. Your speed will be terrible with all this turbulence in the sails, so move the jib lead aft a notch or two.

With a lot of load on the block, it's difficult to make the adjustment on the trimmed sail. Move the block on the inactive jibsheet to where you think it should be. Then tack and allow the boat to settle down. If it looks right and all else stays equal (wind strength and direction), change the old lead to match and tack back. As the wind increases, the boat might feel overpowered again. To depower the sail, you can move the lead back to allow the upper area to luff and spill out some air. As the wind decreases, move the lead forward or ease the sheets.

As you sail off the wind, you want to maintain proper leech tension. However, easing the jibsheet tends to allow the sail to rise up and loosens the leech. To correct this, move the lead forward. This causes the leech to flatten and reduces the twist at the top of the sail. An outboard lead (called a *barberhauler*) attached to the clew of the sail can also help by pulling the sail down, and not in, without changing the slot and the pressure of the wind between the jib and mainsail.

The set of the jib on a close reach is important. It might look full, but the sail might not be

GETTING PAST A FEAR OF WEATHER
• • • • • • • • • • • • • • • • • •

Mimi Starke—a 50-something, 4-foot, 11-inch dynamo who has often appeared as a panelist in NWSA "Take the Helm" seminars—says she copes with weather fears by asking herself, "Is it life threatening, or merely impressive?"

Mimi's introduction to sailing was a disaster. As an adolescent, she took lessons on a small, tippy boat and hated sailing so much her instructor refunded her money. Much later, as a young newlywed, she and her husband started sailing with friends, bought their first of several boats, and started to dream about cruising. In 1992, Mimi, her husband, and their 9-year-old son embarked on a nine-month cruise that changed their lives.

(continued on page 121)

set efficiently. If you ease it out and trim it in periodically as you sail, you'll notice a point where the telltales are drawing equally on both sides of the sail. That's perfect.

As you turn farther off the wind, a genoa or jib becomes less and less a factor in the speed of the boat. Eventually you'll either roll it up or take it down and set a spinnaker or an *asymmetrical spinnaker*, a sail designed for cruising sailors who want to avoid the fuss of setting a spinnaker pole.

On a spinnaker, the luff and leech are the same length. To set a standard spinnaker, a spinnaker pole must be horizontally attached to the mast and to a corner of the sail (the tack). This pole has four lines to adjust it up or down and forward and aft. An asymmetrical spinnaker is made out of the same colorful nylon, but it doesn't have equal length luffs (hence asymmetrical), and it doesn't require the pole to keep its shape.

Underwater dynamics

As the boat sails, water flows along the hull, keel, and rudder. Here, shape and smoothness also affect speed and performance. If there are barnacles or rough areas on the hull, keel, or rudder, water cannot flow smoothly. Turbulence is created, and this slows the boat down.

The keel and rudder are also designed to act like an airfoil. Their *leading edges* (the area where water hits first, divides, and flows past) are usually wider or fatter forward and thinner aft. This keeps disruption of that water flow to a minimum. Beyond their shape and design, another important factor is how clean and smooth these surfaces are.

Successful racing sailors are fastidious about bottom surfaces. Some sand and clean their boat bottom and underwater foils before every race. If you see grass along a boat's waterline, you can bet there's more growing below the waterline: more grass, barnacles, and possibly a rough paint job. With all this, a boat not only looks terrible, it can't possibly reach its optimal speed.

WEATHER AND WIND

Sailing is a combination of human, natural, and mechanical dynamics. To sail intelligently, you should be able to identify wind direction and common weather patterns that occur in your sailing

"The biggest concern women have about sailing is weather. But the more experience you have, the less you tend to worry. When you're out there, you just handle it."

—Barbara Marrett, age 41

area. Using that information, you can make a plan that addresses where you want to sail, the appropriate sails and settings for the conditions, and safety considerations.

The fact is, if you're truly going to enjoy sailing, you can't let potential weather rule every outing. In a perfect world, you'd sail wherever you wanted and always find calm seas and gentle breezes. Every day would be sunny and bright, never too hot or too cold; every night would be starry and clear, with moonlight streaking across the water. Difficult weather conditions are more the exception than the rule. But if you work on your own abilities, you'll have the confidence to handle the challenges of weather without hesitation.

Educate yourself about the weather before you go sailing. Check local forecasts that give you information for the next few hours or several days. Television and radio weather channels are helpful. Some newspaper weather maps can be useful, but only if you compare these over a period of days. Local airport reports are also a source of information. But the best source is the United States National Weather Service, which broadcasts current and expected conditions, with continual updates, over VHF channels. These reports are available on VHF radiotelephones, the marine band on multiband portable radios, radio direction finders, and special weather radios. All of these instruments are line-of-sight, reaching up to 40 miles. That is fine for most of us who sail close to home. For itineraries covering longer distances, a single-sideband radio (SSB) that has a range of several hundred miles is better.

Understanding weather is a huge subject—one too lengthy to cover fully in this book. But the following, using John Rousmaniere's *The Annapolis Book of Seamanship* and *Chapman*

GETTING PAST A FEAR OF WEATHER

(continued from page 120)

Mimi was reluctant to leave solid ground, and it was fear of the weather that nearly kept her ashore. She had to get out and realize how seaworthy her 35-foot Sabre was—and realize how well she could handle the motion, how much her son was enjoying the passage, and how right her husband was to get them underway when they did.

Today, the Starkes are in the boat business on Chesapeake Bay and planning their next cruise. Mimi is a wonderful resource for any woman contemplating a similar journey. It worked for Mimi and her husband because they prepared and considered each other's needs.

Piloting as resources, will give you a basis to work from. (For more weather information sources and seminars for women, see Chapter 10, "Resources.")

Tips for understanding weather

Because weather moves from west to east in the Northern Hemisphere, experienced sailors look to the west to scout out weather changes. They then check their barometers (which read changes in air pressure), radio broadcasts, and weather maps. Dense clouds to the west, gusty winds, and changeable air temperatures indicate deteriorating weather.

Weather systems occur in the first two levels of our atmosphere, which rise no more than 11 miles above the equator and 5 miles above the earth's poles. The sun's radiant energy creates climatic conditions in our atmosphere by clouds, land, and water absorbing or reflecting solar rays. In our hemisphere, local daily weather cycles tend to follow the path of the sun.

How weather creates wind

The sinking and rising of air creates circulation, which combines with the earth's rotation to make weather. A continuous flow of warm and cool air results as warm air rises from the equator and flows toward the poles, while cooler air from the poles flows underneath toward the equator.

Air moving from areas of high pressure to low pressure creates wind. Weather maps show these high pressure and low pressure areas, described by bands (*isobars*) connecting points of equal pressure at various locations. When the isobars are close (steep), this indicates a larger change in pressure with stronger winds. *High-pressure areas* produce less wind and fair weather. *Low-pressure areas* signify heavy or unsettled weather with more wind.

In the Northern Hemisphere, circulation around a high-pressure area is clockwise, with air spinning outward and to the right. Around lows, air is pulled inward in a counterclockwise direction. To find the center of a low and the resulting increase in wind in the Northern Hemisphere—with your back to the wind, the low-pressure area is to your left.

Fronts

A *front* is a boundary between two air masses. *Air masses* are big blobs of air in which temperature and moisture conditions are horizontally the same. Air masses pick up regional temperature and moisture and carry these as they move. For instance, an air mass over central Canada would be cool (because Canada is far to the north) and dry (no water to speak of). An air mass over the Caribbean would be warm and pick up lots of moisture from the warm water. Cold air masses are unstable since they pick up warm air near the earth's surface and try to rise or bubble up through colder air layers. This results in strong gusty winds, and possible cotton-ball-like cumulus clouds.

Warm air masses are relatively stable, with warm air already above the cooler air that is picked up from colder ground levels. Warm air masses carry steady but weaker winds and drizzly rain.

When air masses of different temperatures collide, fronts and storms are created. *Cold fronts* are the most unpredictable, and they travel quickly. In the Northern Hemisphere, they move east to southeast. If you start to feel a cool breeze and the wind shifts to the south when you're sailing on a warm day, a cold front is moving your way. This can rapidly produce high winds and *squalls* (a line of thunderstorms ahead of the approaching front). Dark clouds form on the horizon. If you have a barometer aboard, you'll see it drop. The faster it drops, the stronger the approaching front. The wind will continue shifting clockwise as the front passes, sometimes ending up in the north and northeast and blowing strongly from that direction for a few days.

A *warm front* is more stable and less dramatic. It occurs when warm air reaches and rides over colder air and produces milder weather, low-level dense clouds, and extended light rain. A warm front moves slowly and will eventually be overtaken by a cold front.

An *occluded front* occurs when a warm front is shoved upward by a cold front, rising into high cumulus clouds. If the temperature and humidity differences between the two fronts are great, stormy and unpredictable weather results. Otherwise, the weather will stabilize.

A *stationary front* results when two air masses don't interact because neither is well defined. In this case, weather changes can go either way and little will happen until another air mass arrives on the scene.

Reading clouds

When air is forced upward—either because warm air is overriding cold air, or because the sun is heating up the earth's surface—it cools. Since cold air cannot hold as much water vapor as warmer air, a temperature is eventually reached where the water vapor condenses out into liquid cloud droplets. If the temperature is cold enough, usually above 20,000 feet, ice rather than water forms. Clouds found at about 20,000 feet and higher are made up of ice crystals. Clouds that form at 7,000 to 20,000 feet are made up of water droplets.

Cirrus clouds are the highest, with a thin wispy appearance. They often signify the approach of a warm front.

There's an old saying: Mackerel skies and mares' tails make tall ships carry low sails. When cirrus clouds look like wisps (mares' tails), fair weather is predicted—unless the hairs of the tail point downward or upward, signifying rain.

When the sky is draped in a thin, high cloud layer, a halo of ice crystals is often seen around the sun and a storm is imminent. This is common with cirrostratus clouds, which are wispy and formed in sheets, that develop just under cirrus clouds as a warm front approaches and layers of cold air mix with warm air.

Cirrocumulus clouds, the next layer down, appear in large gray and white clumps of repeated patterns across the sky and portend changeable weather and probable storms. When viewed from below, they can look like fishscales. This is the mackerel sky in the above saying.

When thick, grayish-blue, almost uniform clouds form with a hazy sun peeking through, these are *altostratus*. As they thicken and darken, rain develops.

Altocumulus clouds are the beautiful cotton puffs seen against a deep blue summer sky. With little moisture in the atmosphere, these indicate fair weather, particularly at lower levels. If they get darker and bigger, expect squalls.

Stratocumulus clouds are patchy gray and/or white, with rounded surfaces. When clouds are dark gray, thick, and fairly uniform, this indicates relatively stable air and possibly a steady drizzle.

Cumulonimbus clouds are dark, tightly packed balls at about 6,000 feet that can churn and develop into ominous thunderheads created by violent updrafts moving through a wide range of temperatures. As they build vertically, they combine elements from several different layers and form towers or mounds. The top parts look like a cauliflower and are pure white when lit by the sun; their bottoms are usually dark, horizontal, and ragged. When an anvil head appears—which is broader than the base—winds are strong and threatening. Expect more violent conditions with sharper edges and darker color.

Cumulus clouds, which are puffy and white, are generally associated with fair weather. When cruising in the Caribbean, almost every island has a cloud over its peak. These cumulus clouds indicate rising thermals (air heated by the warmer land). In our hemisphere, they indicate a good sea breeze. When cumulus clouds darken and enlarge, they usually develop into cumulonimbus thunderheads, with an advent of squalls in less than two hours.

From ground to 7,000 feet, dark gray *nimbostratus* clouds can form a dark blanket and obscure the sun just before a steady downpour. Associated with warm fronts, sometimes their bases are so close to the ground they can be confused with heavy fog.

The lowest layer—*stratus clouds*—are low and flat, with minimal precipitation in the form of an occasional light drizzle.

When sailing near home, expect weather changes if cloud color, shape, and size change. In general, isolated, wispy, white, high clouds indicate good, steady weather. Dark, dense, crowded, towering clouds suggest changing weather—usually for the worse, including rain and squalls.

You can spot rain areas by a gray veil that extends from a cloud and obscures the horizon. If it's straight down, there's not much wind; if slanted, you can determine which way it's moving and avoid getting wet.

Fog

This strange phenomenon makes sailing very mysterious, if not a little scary. In the hushed atmosphere surrounding your boat, bell buoys and large ships can suddenly appear out of nowhere. When air is saturated with water (called the *dew point*) and local conditions cool the air to its dew point, fog develops. An example of this occurs when damp sea or lake air flows across cold water. Fog can appear on land when the air is suddenly cooled at sunset, at sea when cold water currents meet warm moist air, and in the morning when cold air sinks and cools the air over a river or lake. Until it's reheated by the sun or a large land mass, fog can hang around for quite a while.

Since fog is difficult to predict without an instrument that measures the dew point of air, it's best to know how to cope with fog when it rolls in. (Some of these steps involve basic navigation, which you'll learn about in Chapter 8.)

"**W**e got caught on our second cruise in gale-force winds and ten-foot seas. After praying, I concentrated on everything I ever learned about heavy weather and about the integrity of our boat. It worked."

—Jane Candella, age 49

1.   Get your bearings. Determine where you are and where the nearest safe harbor is as soon as the first sign of fog appears.

2.   Slow down to minimum speed and, if possible, anchor away from any areas of boating activity (such as shipping lanes).

3.   Maintain a lookout for lights and sounds, such as foghorns or other vessels, and keep updating your bearings when you can see buoys or landmarks.

4.   Use sound signals to warn others of your presence. If you're underway, use a foghorn to sound one long blast followed by two short blasts. If you're at anchor, ring a bell for five seconds every minute; in addition, make one short blast—one long blast—one short blast at intervals to alert any approaching vessels.

Lightning and sailing

A greater concern to many sailors is lightning. While few boats are hit, it can happen. Most sailboats are grounded by a wire that connects the bottom of the mast to the keel. Grounding helps reduce the charge difference between the boat and the cloud, reducing the likelihood of lightning hitting the mast.

What do you do if you're caught in a lightning storm? If visibility is pretty good and you're in home waters, try to get back to port. If you can't see anything, hazards such as breakwaters might be the bigger problem. In any case, note your position as the storm begins. Take bearings and get a fix of where you are,

HAVING A PLAN

Thinking through the steps you should take as bad weather approaches will help you develop a logical plan for handling the conditions. Here are some guidelines.

- Figure out where you are. Take bearings; be aware of any hazards or other boats you can see in your path.

- Determine where the nearest safe harbor is. How long will it take you to get there? How difficult or easy is the approach?

- Head for home or to that safe harbor—whichever is closest. If that destination is surrounded by shoal waters, weigh the merits of staying out and "weathering the storm" versus getting into tricky navigation areas in poor visibility.

- Reduce or change sails if heavy air is anticipated (before the heavy air gets to you).

- Pull out your foul-weather gear and warmer clothes and put them in a handy location.

- Put your life vest and safety harness on (if you're on a larger boat and have one) over your foul-weather gear.

- Check your anchor and rode; make sure it can run freely.

(continued on page 126)

HAVING A PLAN

(continued from page 125)

- Tie down anything that could fly off the boat and, on larger boats, make sure everything is stowed well below.

- On larger boats with navigation lights, turn these on if a dark storm is imminent.

- Make sure your safety equipment is easy to reach.

- If you have an engine, be prepared to turn it on. This can help you control the boat if winds are very strong and you need to get your sails completely down.

- Stay calm and give clear directions to your crew and passengers. Assure them you are ready for what's coming.

then calculate your compass heading back to safety (you'll learn about navigation in Chapter 8).

If it's wiser to wait out the storm and you can anchor, do it. If you're out in deep water where anchoring is out of the question, you can sail back and forth in short distances on a reach or heave-to to stay in the same general location.

During the storm, avoid touching two areas simultaneously that can conduct electricity (like a stay and the mast). Stay out of the water and below if possible. Most storms pass quickly. Before you know it, the sun will come out and your foul-weather gear will be hanging on the rail to dry.

Effect of local conditions on weather patterns

Many factors affect wind direction and speed near land. When an *onshore breeze* (breeze blowing from a body of water to shore) approaches a steep area of land, it might start to lift way offshore to get over that bluff. When the breeze is blowing from the land toward the body of water, this is called an *offshore breeze*. In this situation, the offshore breeze blowing over the bluff usually creates a calm area near shore that is ideal for anchoring, but not for sailing!

Wind can be channeled down city streets, through valleys, and between two points of land, creating a blast near shore in these vicinities.

In warmer weather, land heats up as the day goes on while the water temperature remains the same. As the air heats it rises, and cooler air from the water moves in underneath to create a *sea breeze*, usually a delightful wind sailors look for in the late afternoon to fill in offshore and move towards the land. When the land cools off at night, the system reverses, creating a land breeze that blows from the land to the water.

Thunderheads often develop in late summer afternoons, when cold and warm air of significantly different temperatures collide and force the warmer, moist air rapidly upward. The very top, plume-shaped crown of that cumulonimbus cloud leans toward the direction the upper wind is blowing and tells you the direction the storm is moving in. As a thunderstorm approaches, the wind ahead might be variable or steady. The leading edge of the storm—a roll cloud formed by violent air currents—brings with it heavy shifting winds and strong downdrafts that carry lightning. Just behind it is heavy rain and hail. After it passes, you'll feel cooler, less humid temperatures. If the thunderhead is low, or the roll cloud and the plume way up high are not developed, the storm is less likely to be severe.

Squalls and local storms might not all result from a front. Sometimes you'll see dark clouds approach and you are hit in a matter of minutes with a blast of wind and pelting rain. Then it's gone, skies are sunny, and the wind is calm.

> "The best experience I had was sailing under the Verrazano Bridge in a driving rainstorm. It was exhilarating, especially when we saw the clouds break and sun shine on the skyline. What an accomplishment!"
>
> —Dolores Bittleman, age 66

In warmer climates, water spouts can form, but they are rare. I was caught in one at our sailing school on Captiva Island, in Florida. I noticed a tiny spur that extended down from low, dark clouds, and saw it connect with the water to form a column between the water and the cloud. As it approached, we got our sails down and anchored. It hit and was gone in what seemed like an instant, leaving us becalmed and pointing 180 degrees from our original heading at anchor.

Another phenomenon can occur in a cloudless sky. Commonly referred to as a *white squall*, it hits with a blast of wind for a very brief period of time, and it is also relatively rare.

The best-known sailors' adage goes: Red sky in morning, sailors take warning; red sky at night, sailors' delight. A red sunset or dawn is caused by the sun's rays shining through dust particles in clear, dry air. Since this is in the west at night, you can expect good weather. When it occurs in the morning, with the sun to the east, this indicates the good weather has passed and the next cycle will probably bring rain.

I can count on one hand the number of times I've experienced threatening weather while sailing. Most of the time, the weather is fine, more often with less wind than I like. Sailboats can take just about anything; it's us gals (and guys) who are fragile. Good common sense, the knowledge to anticipate local conditions, proper planning, and ability to make the boat and yourself more comfortable when conditions deteriorate all make the difference.

Wind strengths

Wind strength is measured in knots. One knot equals 1.15 statute miles. Sailors use the Beaufort Scale, which reflects wind and sea conditions offshore over large bodies of water. The higher the force, the more severe the conditions are. Created in 1805 by the British admiral Sir Francis Beaufort, it doesn't necessarily reflect the conditions we experience in areas surrounded by or close to land.

As a new sailor, you will probably overestimate how strong the wind really is and how high the waves really are. This is normal. Sailboats can take a lot of wind. The stronger the wind while you're learning, the more capable and confident you'll be later on. Hopefully, you'll experience a

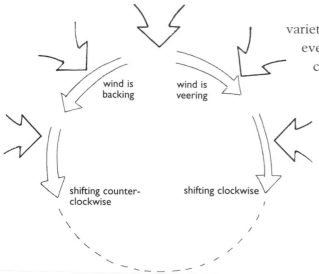

wind is backing

wind is veering

shifting counter-clockwise

shifting clockwise

When the wind shifts counterclockwise, it's called **backing**. When it shifts clockwise, it's called **veering**.

variety of conditions with your instructor. Then, if you're ever out there when it gets up over 25 knots, you'll consider it just another challenge.

WIND SHIFTS AND HOW TO USE THEM

Racing sailors are constantly on the lookout for puffs on the water, or looking at the set of other sailboats' sails on the horizon. Anticipating a change in wind direction or strength before your competitor does is often the difference between winning and losing a race.

Smart sailors watch for wind shifts that will put them on a shorter course to their destination. Learn to anticipate changes and use them to your advantage—or at least avoid any disadvantages, such as having too much sail up when a stronger wind fills in, or putting a nice lunch out in the cockpit just when the wind shifts and sails need to be trimmed.

The two most important features to understand about a wind shift are the direction it comes from and what effect it will have when it reaches you.

When the wind shifts in a clockwise direction, it's called *veering*. When it shifts counterclockwise, it's called *backing*. The wind can also shift back and forth fairly consistently, but still maintain the same mean direction. This is an *oscillating* wind. If the tendency is for the mean wind direction to travel to the left or the right, it becomes a *continual shift* and will affect the distance you need to travel to get back home.

Learn to watch for clues about the wind: how smoke flows from a smokestack ashore; the set of another sailboat's sails. Telltale dark patches and ripples on the water can also indicate new wind (some ripples can also come from current and shallow water). As the wind shifts and fills in from a different direction, these dark patches become more persistent and get bigger and bigger—until they are all around you and the wind settles down from a new direction.

Many factors affect wind shifts and wind direction: the temperature of the water relative to the temperature of the air; the height and shape of the terrain around you; weather patterns; and where you are on the planet. The more you sail, the more you will learn about weather patterns and how to recognize them.

Acting on the clues around you

Smart sailors continually observe the wind and weather around them. When they see signs of a change, they take their best course of action. Here are some examples of the kinds of things that can tip you off to changes in wind strength and direction and how these changes affect you.

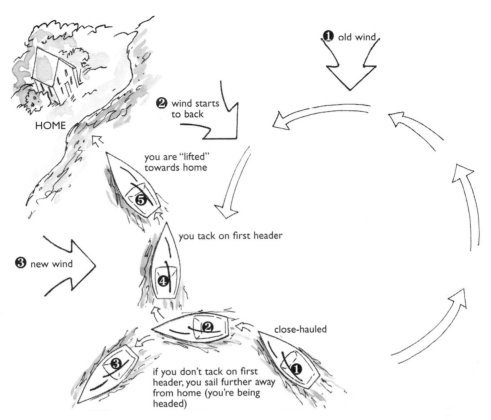

❶ old wind

❷ wind starts to back

HOME

you are "lifted" towards home

❺

you tack on first header

❸ new wind

❹

close-hauled

❷

❸

if you don't tack on first header, you sail further away from home (you're being headed)

❶

When the wind starts to back, you're being **headed**. You should tack on a header for the shortest course to your destination, and you'll be lifted toward home. Position (**1**) shows the boat closehauled on a port tack. As the wind backs, the boat starts to sail away from home (**2**) and is being headed badly (**3**). If you tacked right after you were headed (**4**), you 'd be lifted on a nearly straight course to home (**5**).

- You left the harbor in a moderate breeze, with an offshore wind at your back. It's a beautiful day, and although you seem to be going slower and slower, you don't mind—nor do you notice a sailboat on the horizon coming toward you on the same tack you're on! That boat is telling you that the wind is 180 degrees different out where that other boat is. You keep sailing. Suddenly, you run out of wind and the afternoon seabreeze fills in. You turn to head home; you are now sailing downwind, on a slow point of sail and running out of time. If you have an engine, you turn it on. If you're on a small boat with no auxiliary power, you just take it on the chin and arrive late. Had you planned for the prevailing wind pattern, or noticed the boat ahead coming at you on the same tack, you might have turned to go back earlier and arrived with time to spare.

- You're sailing along on a beat, enjoying a great afternoon breeze. Your destination is ahead, slightly to port. You notice more and more wind shifts coming in from the left. Each of these shifts is a header, which means you have to fall off. You are on starboard tack, and you fall off with each shift—your bow falling farther away from your destination. But you could have taken a different action: you could have taken a tack when the first header hit. If you did that, you'd be on the *lifted* tack—and you'd sail a shorter distance to your destination upwind.

- We were racing in England in the 1979 Cowes Week, held off the Isle of Wight. In the last race held before the start of the Fastnet Race—an offshore race that lasts several days—we were in second place, just behind the America's Cup sailor Ted Turner. I began to notice boats behind us broaching badly (being forced over on their sides and out of control). This indicated very strong wind was coming, but we could taste victory and were loath to take down any sails or take in any reefs. Although we had plenty of warning, we ended up on our side—like a wallowing whale with our third spreader near the top of the mast in the water. Having blown out most of our headsails, we abandoned the race and sailed in to have them repaired. We didn't heed the warning, but we did have a twist of fate: a savage storm ravaged the fleet in the 1979 Fastnet Race. Winds reached over 80 knots and fifteen people died. Those repaired sails were our salvation in the extremely challenging conditions. We also won our division.

USE OF CREW WEIGHT AND PLACEMENT

Some boats are more sensitive than others when it comes to how crew weight is distributed. The shape of the hull and keel might also determine where the crew should sit.

Many modern boats are far lighter and more sensitive to crew weight than older designs. Some racing sailboats are designed to go very fast downwind, and they are constructed out of exotic, ultralight materials with flatter bottoms and less weight in the keel. On these boats, you're extremely concerned with how much weight you put aboard and where you sit during a race—in addition to paying attention to how the sails are trimmed.

For example, on a run in light air, you might move the crew weight aft to prevent the bow from burying. If work needs to be done anywhere forward of the mast, the lightest person gets the job. In very light wind, on any point of sail, sudden maneuvers or quick actions can spill the wind out of the sails, so everyone should take care to move as little as possible. If there's a lot of wind, a boat sailing downwind or on a broad reach will start to *surf* off the waves with increased speed. To maintain this speed, shift crew weight aft as the boat scoots down the wave and forward as it climbs up the wave, in preparation for the next burst of speed.

Unless you're racing and pushing the boat to the max, you're not apt to encounter this type of sailing. Cruising boats are built for comfort and stability—with roomy interiors and large cockpits for lounging around. Rarely do you worry about where you sit or what you bring aboard on a cruising boat. But if you're invited to be part of a racing machine, say yes—and see what excitement sailing really can bring!

Chapter 8

NAVIGATION RULES AND TECHNIQUES

Navigation is one of the most important jobs on a sailboat. Most beginning courses give you enough instruction to sail in local waters. You can also take piloting (coastal navigation) courses provided by your local Power Squadron (check nearby marinas and clubs), home-study courses advertised in sailing magazines, and special courses from commercial sailing schools (certification is available through those offering the US SAILING Coastal Navigation course). NWSA gives several women-only weekend workshops each year; these hands-on sessions are run while students sail on a 125-foot schooner.

The information that follows will get you started. But if you're serious about sailing beyond your home waters, plan on going further. If you start sailing out of sight of land, where there are no buoys or markers to guide your way, you'll also want to learn celestial navigation (based on reading the positions of stars, moon, sun) as a backup for the many electronic devices you'll probably have aboard.

KNOW THE RULES

Just as a set of rules govern how we drive on our roads, a set of rules govern how boaters should transit through the waterways. The United States abides by the International Rules, which were originally approved by Great Britain in 1884, adopted and amended by an act of U.S. Congress

• •

"I do much better with navigation and
problem solving than my husband."

—Suzanne Rummel, age 54

• •

in 1885, and universally effective on January 1, 1954. The section relating to collisions is called Navigation Rules, and it encompasses all vessels (powerboats, sailboats, and seaplanes). These have been revised and simplified over the years to their present form and are available in any store that carries books on boating. You should commit them to memory and have a copy of the book aboard, if you intend to keep on sailing.

There are no road signs on the water. But there are numbered channel markers, buoys, and nuns (cone-shaped floats) that are color-coded. They mark where to go and what to avoid.

A *channel* is the equivalent of a highway on land: the channel, marked by buoys, is the route boats use to transit in and out of harbors. There are rules about what side of the channel you use to enter and leave a port. Every new sailor in the United States has probably heard the saying, "red, right, returning." When you're coming into a harbor, or sailing from a larger body of water to a smaller one, keep the red channel markers or buoys on your right (starboard) side. Make note that this works fine in the United States; but in international waters, it's the reverse.

Another rule covers what side to stay on as you pass other boats in a channel. Like driving in the United States, you generally stay to the right side of the road. On the water, pass port-to-port: each boat keeps the approaching boat on its port side and keeps the outside edge of the channel on its starboard side.

Who has the right of way?

How do you know who has right of way when two boats approach each other? Who must do what to avoid a collision? How do you know if you're on a collision course?

You should have a compass aboard. This is not only used to determine your heading, but it also helps you determine your position with respect to other boats and objects. If you sight along the compass (*take a bearing*) on an approaching boat or object and that bearing does not change when checked several times over a short period of time, you must assume there is a risk of collision and be prepared to alter your course. If you take a bearing on a boat that is approaching on your port side and that bearing moves forward (clockwise), you might assume the other boat will pass ahead of you; if it moves aft (counterclockwise), you will pass ahead. If you take a bearing on a boat that is approaching on your starboard side and the bearing moves forward (counterclockwise), the other boat will pass ahead; if it moves aft (clockwise), you will pass ahead.

Without a compass, you can take this bearing by lining up the other boat with a stanchion (or some other vertical part on your boat). If the boat or object doesn't move relative to the stanchion, you might be on a collision course. If it moves ahead of the stanchion, it will pass ahead of you. If the bearing moves behind the stanchion, you'll pass ahead.

You've determined you are on a collision course with another boat. Which one has to alter course? Here are the rules:

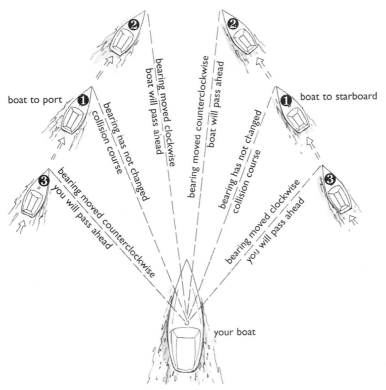

To determine if you're on a collision course with another boat, take bearings from your compass or sight along a stanchion on your boat. If the bearing doesn't change (1), you're on a collision course. If the bearing on a boat to port moves clockwise—or on a boat to starboard moves counterclockwise—that boat will pass ahead of yours (2). If the bearing moves counterclockwise on a boat to port—or clockwise on a boat to starboard—you'll pass ahead of the other boat (3).

● When two sailboats are approaching one another, regardless of your point of sail, the rules are determined by what tack you are on (starboard or port): if you're on the same tack, which boat is to windward or leeward of the other; if you're going in the same direction, which boat is overtaking the other. These rules apply only if both boats are sailing and not using an engine.

1. A sailboat on port tack must keep clear of a sailboat on starboard tack. In other words, the starboard-tack boat has right of way. Think of starboard as *right*—your right to keep on sailing without having to alter your course.

2. When two sailboats are on the same tack, the boat to windward must keep clear of the boat to leeward. The leeward boat has right of way.

3. When a sailboat is overtaking another, it must avoid the boat ahead.

Remember this helpful phrase: POWs never have rights—*p*ort tack, *o*vertaking, *w*indward boats.

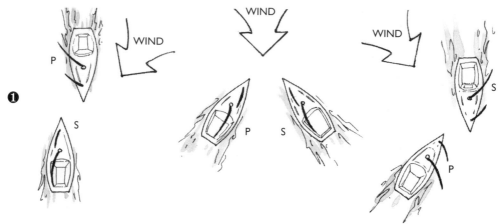

A sailboat on a port tack (**P**) must keep clear of a sailboat on a starboard tack (**S**). Starboard tack boat has the right of way.

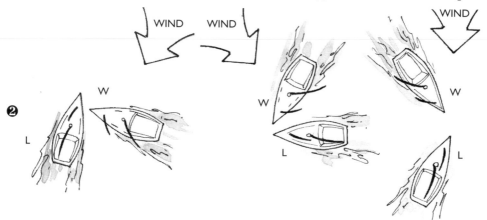

When two sailboats are on the same tack, the boat to the windward (**W**) must keep clear of the boat to leeward (**L**). Leeward has the right of way.

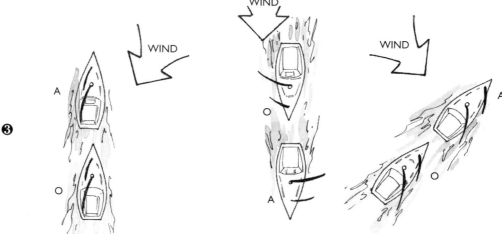

When a sailboat is overtaking another (**O**), it must avoid the boat ahead (**A**).

Right of way rules, both boats under sail.

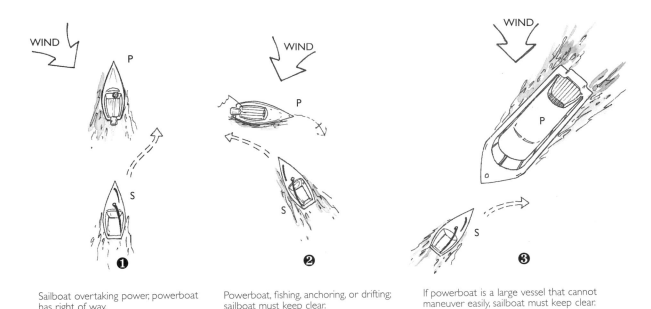

① Sailboat overtaking power; powerboat has right of way.

② Powerboat, fishing, anchoring, or drifting; sailboat must keep clear.

③ If powerboat is a large vessel that cannot maneuver easily, sailboat must keep clear.

Right of way rules, sailboat and powerboat approaching.

- When a sailboat and power-driven boat are approaching one another, the boat under sail alone usually has right of way. Exceptions occur when:

  1. The sailboat is overtaking the powerboat.

  2. The powerboat is fishing, anchored, or drifting (no one in command).

  3. The powerboat is a large vessel that cannot maneuver easily.

  In areas where there are shipping channels, sailboats must always get out of the way of large commercial vessels. When in doubt, be prudent; alter your course before it's too late. And watch for ships towing barges, where the tow might be very far back or the ship might have slowed down to allow the towline to drag below the water. There are horror stories about sailboats and powerboats that tried to pass between a ship and its tow, with considerable damage and loss of life.

- When any two boats are approaching, both under power, the boat in the other's *danger zone* has right of way. The danger zone is defined as the area from dead ahead to two points abaft the starboard beam (from the tip of the bow to 22.5 degrees behind the middle point of the boat on its starboard side).

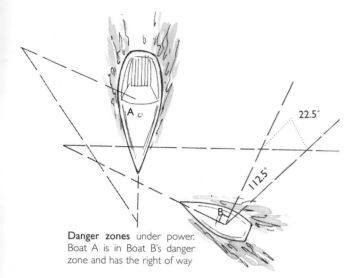

Danger zones under power. Boat A is in Boat B's danger zone and has the right of way

Remember that a sailboat can have an engine. So this rule also applies to two sailboats when they are both using their engines, as well as to a powerboat and a sailboat under power—even if the sailboat(s) in either case have their sails up and appear to be sailing.

When you first start sailing, you might not venture out at night. But you could get caught out there with no wind when dusk falls, so you'll need to know about lights. Unless your boat has them, be very prudent about getting back home in plenty of daylight.

- To determine if a boat is in your danger zone at night, watch for the following combinations:

    1. If you see a red and a green light and two white (range) lights in line (one higher than the other), this indicates that the boat is heading toward you and you are either in danger of colliding or you might not be able to cross that boat. If the range lights are not in line and the lower bow light is to the right of the higher range light, this indicates that the boat is probably moving to your right. If the lower range light is to the left of the bow light, this indicates that the boat is moving to your left.

    2. If you see a green side light, you should be free and clear. Either the other boat is on a parallel course to yours, is going to pass behind you, or has already crossed your bow and is moving away from you.

    3. If you see a low white light, you are probably staring at the boat's stern. If you are moving faster, you must stay clear while overtaking it.

    4. If you see a red light, watch out. You might be on a collision course, and since the other boat is in your danger zone, you must avoid any possibility of a collision.

There are many times at night when you'll see lights of other boats that might not be in your danger zone but could still cause a threat if not watched. The tug and tow are a case in point. Think how difficult it would be to stop a tug if you started to sail between the tug and the tow. People who run commercial boats and ships tend to assume everyone else knows what their lights mean and will get out of their way.

Night sailing is romantic. But before you agree to share an evening in the moonlight from the deck of a moving sailboat, find out if your date or anyone else aboard is experienced at sail-

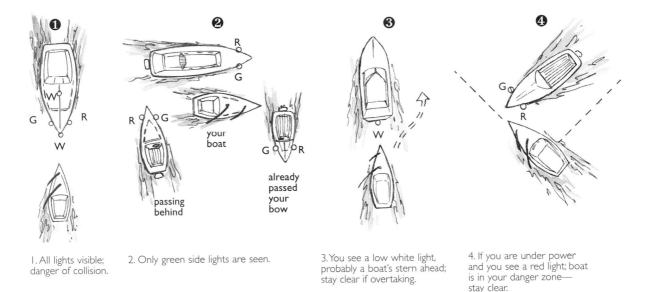

1. All lights visible; danger of collision.

2. Only green side lights are seen.

3. You see a low white light, probably a boat's stern ahead; stay clear if overtaking.

4. If you are under power and you see a red light; boat is in your danger zone—stay clear.

Danger zones at night.

ing in the dark. Nothing can compare to sailing along under a myriad of stars in a velvet sky, a glass of bubbly in one hand, the soft summer-night breeze in your hair, that someone you really like by your side. . . . But suddenly, the throbbing noise of approaching engines and a dark shadow seem to come out of nowhere, with lights neither you nor your date understand. Be the smart one: Study the Navigation Rules—and don't sail at night until you know them.

THE BASIC STEPS OF NAVIGATION

If you sail small boats off the beach or in protected harbors—and that's all you plan to do—you probably won't get deeply into navigation. If you do go aground, you can easily step off the boat and push yourself free.

But most women getting involved in sailing these days would rather be comfortable than wet, and they prefer to sail on larger boats. Knowing how to read a chart, figure out where you are, and chart a course are all very important. Even if you have no intention of owning a boat and plan to sail with friends, rent near home, or charter in exotic places, I doubt you'll want to depend on others to tell you where you are and where to go. Some women think you have to be great with numbers to be a good navigator: not true. All you need is the desire to know where you are and where you're going.

Tools you'll need

The basic tools of coastal navigation are proper charts for the area, a pair of parallel rulers, dividers, pencils, a pencil sharpener, and a reliable compass. If you sail on larger boats, you'll also use electronic instruments that read the depth of the water, calculate drift due to currents, indi-

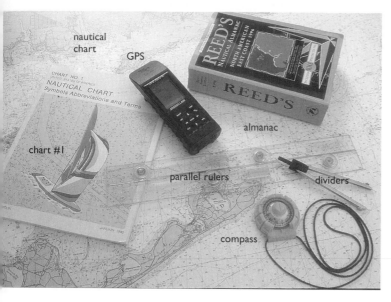

Navigation tools.

cate your speed-made-good over the bottom and the distance you've sailed, and pinpoint your spot on the globe.

In this computer age, a handheld GPS is more and more the instrument of choice aboard. This neat little tool is programmed to find your location with the aid of satellites through the Global Positioning System. You should always back up these electronic readings with chart work and compass bearings. The satellite system is managed by the Department of Defense for the U.S. armed forces and its allies. In the event of any threat, the satellite constellation providing information to handheld receivers will be shut down for all but the military.

If you have a large-enough boat and pocketbook to put all the bells and whistles aboard, you'll definitely want: a *depth sounder*, to measure the depth of water under your keel; a *radar*, an electronic device that shows the position, size, and distance of objects around you (especially valuable at night and in bad visibility); a *fixed GPS* (as opposed to a handheld model); a *weather fax*, which allows you to receive weather maps by fax; and other instruments to help you navigate and predict the weather.

How to read a chart

Our waterways are marked with aids that tell us where to find channels, and where to avoid rocks, sunken hazards, reefs, and shoal water. These aids are noted on nautical charts. Charts are produced in the United States by the Department of Commerce, through NOAA (National Oceanic and Atmospheric Administration), and around the world by several other national authorities. In addition to these official documents, there are private companies that produce navigational materials (like the ChartKit series) that help guide you through inland waterways.

A chart is simply a map of a body of water. However, sailors never refer to them as

Learning to use a chart: measuring the distance between two buoys (using dividers) and determining the compass course for getting from one buoy to the other. The parallel rulers are lined up through the two buoys and "walked" to center of compass rose to get the reading.

maps: the proper term is *chart*. Charts are highly detailed, topographical drawings that show: land elevations and landmarks (such as lighthouses, smoke stacks, towns, and other conspicuous marks); water depths and the nature of the bottom; the location of rocks, wrecks, and shoals; information on tides and currents; and compass heading. Some charts show current directions. *Large-scale charts* include compass variation in the compass rose, which speeds up your calculations (as you'll see later in this chapter). Although charts are usually the same overall size, they are available in different scales and are magnified for harbors and areas with greater hazards. *Small-scale charts* with less detail cover more area and are typically used for planning longer passages.

Make sure you have all the appropriate charts for the areas you intend to sail in. NOAA charts are available at most nautical supply stores. ChartKits can be bought wherever sailing books are sold.

Every line, symbol, and color on a chart provides useful information. Water is shown as white for deep water, light blue for water that is usually less than 20 feet deep, and green for areas that are above water at low tide. Dry land is beige. Scattered throughout the water areas are numbers indicating the depth at mean low water. In some areas, extreme tides can be lower than these numbers, so visual and electronic checks are

"I'm looking forward to safe exploration of coastlines—near and distant."

—Jeanine Careri, age 43

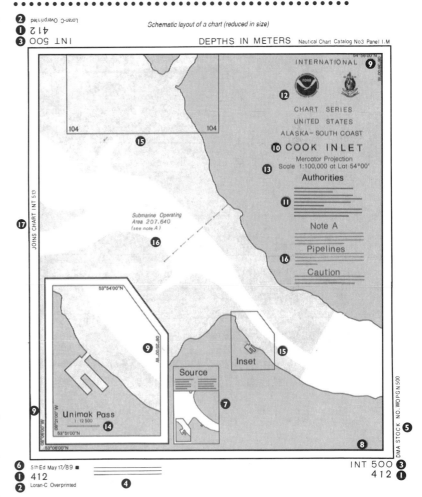

Key features of a nautical chart: 1. Chart number in national chart series; 2. Identification of latticed chart; 3. Chart number in international chart series; 4. Publication note; 5. Stock number; 6. Edition note; 7. Source data diagram; 8. Dimensions of inner borders; 9. Corner co-ordinates; 10. Chart title; 11. Explanatory notes on chart construction, etc.; 12. Seals; 13. Projection and scale of chart at stated latitude; 14. Linear scale on large-scale charts; 15. Reference to larger scale chart; 16. Cautionary notes; 17. Reference to an adjoining chart of similar scale.

prudent. Long, wavy lines show continuous areas of the same depth; these are called *contour lines*. In the beige land areas are a number of objects visible from the water that can be used to take bearings, such as tanks, spires, obvious buildings, lighthouses, and towers.

In addition to numbers for depth, you'll also see symbols with numbers in quotes alongside. The symbols indicate various markers. Buoys are small colored diamonds—red, black, green, black and white, or all white—corresponding to their actual color. A circle underneath indicates their exact location; the number next to it, in quotes, is the number actually written on the buoy. Purple surrounding the diamond or a purple ellipse attached to a black dot indicates a lighted buoy. Red buoys are

Using dividers on a chart to measure distance. Spread tips of dividers from one buoy to the other and, without changing angle between these tips, move the tips to the edge of the chart and count the number of minutes of latitude between the tips. (1 minute = 1 nautical mile)

even-numbered; all others are odd-numbered. Additional information on the chart tells you what type of noise a buoy makes: a bell, gong, or whistle.

Some channels are marked with red triangles or green squares on stakes. On charts, these are usually placed quite close together, with two dotted black lines marking the path from one set to another.

For example, as we leave our canal on Sanibel, Florida, we can look across San Carlos Bay to a flashing white light. On the chart, this is shown as a purple ellipse with a black dot. Written next to it is: Fl 4sec 15ft "23." This tells me it's buoy number 23, with a light flashing every 4 seconds, 15 feet above the water. Near this buoy are two markers, a red triangle marked R"14" and green square marked G"13A." These are numbered channel markers.

Distances on a chart are in nautical miles, and you can measure distances with dividers. Along the sides of the chart are increments that represent minutes of latitude, divided into tenths. Lines of latitude are the horizontal lines around the earth, starting with the equator, that divide it into 360 equal parts of 60 nautical miles each. With 60 minutes to a degree, one nautical mile equals one minute of latitude.

Along the top and bottom of a chart are increments that measure lines of longitude. These lines represent the distances between meridians of longitude that run north and south around the earth and pass through the two poles. They are generally not used when plotting courses.

To measure distance between two points, place a divider tip on each of the two points on the chart. Without changing the angle of the dividers, carry them to nearest side of the chart at the same latitude. Place the two tips in this lined area, with one tip right on a dark or light line.

Then count the number of increments between the two tips. Each of the dark and light sections is a minute, divided into tenths. If the distance measures 5.1 minutes, the distance is 5.1 nautical miles. Be sure to use the scale at the same latitude where you took the reading, because a minute of latitude can be a different measure at different latitudes.

Boat speed is measured in knots, which is the number of nautical miles sailed in an hour. Therefore, you never describe speed in knots per hour. Suppose you want to know how fast you were going when you covered that 5.1 nautical-mile distance that you measured with your dividers. It took you one hour to travel between those two points, so you were sailing at a rate of 5.1 knots.

When distances are greater than the spread of your dividers, take a workable measurement along the edge, set your dividers on this distance, and "walk" the dividers between one point to the other. Count the number of times (legs) you rotate the dividers' position. Then multiply by the number of miles (minutes of latitude) you chose. When you get to the last section, if that last leg is shorter, squeeze the points of the dividers together to fit the space, measure this separately, and add it to your total.

How to use the compass

The compass is essential to locating your position or plotting a course. You'll find a compass rose printed on most charts. It is one circle inside another, with both circles divided into 360 degrees. The outer circle gives you *true* compass direction. The inner circle gives you *magnetic* readings, which is the true heading adjusted by the variation in that location.

As you read your compass, you must consider two factors: *variation* and *deviation*.

Variation is the difference between the geographic meridian (a line passing through the North and South Poles) and the local magnetic meridian (a line running through both magnetic poles). There are only a few places on earth where there's no difference between the magnetic and true poles. On every chart you'll find the number of degrees of variation for that area, which are usually written in the center of the compass rose. This changes each year, so you'll also find a number to indicate the rate of annual change, which is so negligible it can usually be ignored.

You can also see the variation in a given area by noting the difference between the compass readings on the two circles on the chart. Although this doesn't usually amount to much, always consider the age of the chart and the rate of change before using it.

Compasses are affected by metal on the boat. Put a metal can opener directly on a compass, and the needle moves. *Deviation* is the amount the compass needle points to one side or the other of magnetic north. When a new compass is placed aboard a large boat, it must be adjusted. It looks like a lot of hocus pocus, but using magnets and driving the boat in circles, an adjuster can take most of the error out of the compass. He or she can then provide you with a deviation table that shows the difference between the direction the needle should point and the direction it actually points, at different headings. The adjuster took variation into account for this exercise, so if the error is just a few degrees, you usually can take all your compass readings on the inner (magnetic) circle without having to do additional calculations.

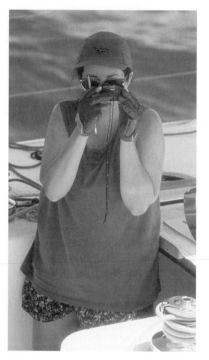

Taking bearings with a **hand-bearing compass**.

You can adjust your own compass by taking readings on known headings, comparing these to the readings on your compass, and use magnets to take out the error.

To remember how to adjust for variation and deviation, expressed as either easterly or westerly errors, use this popular memory jogger: CADET, Compass *Add East for True*. If you know your compass heading, *add* any easterly combined compass errors to obtain the true heading. If you add easterly errors, subtract westerly errors. If you know your true course and want to know what compass course to steer, subtract easterly errors and add westerly errors. For example, your compass reads 090 degrees. The variation on your chart is 15 degrees east and the deviation on your boat at that heading is 5 degrees west. The combined error is 10 degrees east. Your true course, therefore, is 100 degrees.

Determine your position

As you sail along, note buoys and other landmarks. That way, when it's time to take bearings on something ashore or on a navigational aid, you'll know what you're looking at.

To *find your position*, take two *bearings*. Preferably, these should be about 90 degrees apart. You can use a hand-bearing compass or your mounted compass. However, take these as quickly as possible because positions change as the boat moves. Sight on the object that's off your stern or bow first; the angle will change the least if you keep on the same heading. Quickly sight across the compass you steer with, or through a hand-bearing compass, to get the bearing abeam.

Compasses are mounted with the lubber line (fore and aft) in line with your bow. To take an accurate reading on a landmark or object ahead, simply point your bow at that object, even if you have to alter your course slightly to get it dead ahead.

Then take a fix quickly on the object off your beam, note the time to the nearest minute and write all this down. Lay your parallel rulers along the first bearing on the compass rose, walk it to the object you took the fix on, and draw a line right through it. Do the same for the second fix. Your position at the time you took the readings is where the two lines cross. Write the time of that fix next to the intersection in nautical time, which is based on the 24-hour clock. If you took your fix when you woke up that morning at 7:00, then write 0700 on the chart. In nautical time, 1200 is 12 noon, 1300 is 1:00 P.M., 1400 is 2:00 P.M., and so on. Midnight is 0000, and the cycle then begins again with 0100 (1:00 A.M.).

Compass headings are always written in three numbers on the chart, with a zero in front if the number is less than 100 (i.e., 090 for 90 degrees). You probably will be using a chart with a magnetic compass rose and your courses will always be magnetic. But if not, you should indicate M or T (for magnetic or true) to avoid any confusion for someone else navigating with you.

Always try to get close enough to a buoy to read its number. Buoys and channel markers often look alike, and it's easy to think you're at a particular spot. But if you're wrong, you might get into trouble later.

To figure out the distance you need to travel to get to your destination, there's another formula involving distance, speed, and time that's very helpful. If you know two of the variables, the third can be calculated. Use the equation D divided by S times T, which translates to distance (D) divided by speed (S) multiplied by time (T). Put your thumb over the factor you want to find, and what remains is the formula to get there. If you want to find your speed, cover the S and D/T remains. Divide distance by time, and you get speed.

Plot a course

Now that you confirmed where you were at a given time, it's important to monitor where you are going: to constantly update your position relative to the course you wish to sail.

To plot your course, lay the edge of your parallel rulers on your position and your destination. Then "walk" the parallel rulers until one edge passes through the X at the center of the compass rose. Take the compass reading on the magnetic (inner) circle where the parallel ruler edge crosses. That's the course you should be sailing, but lots of factors affect your actual heading and when you'll get to your destination—not the least of which are wind shifts and current.

You shouldn't assume you are where you thought you'd be without visual and calculated verification. As you sail, constantly update your position by calculating your course and distance from your last position.

The lines made by intersecting bearings on a chart are called *lines of position* (LOP), and the spot where they cross is the *fix*. Two or more compass bearings are needed for a fix. One of your bearings can be taken without using a compass if you pass two points of land that line up. Draw a line between these two points and extend it until it meets, or comes very close to, your compass bearings. Note the time you took this bearing between the two points on the chart. When three bearings cross, you usually get a small triangle and can estimate your position to be in the middle. Each time you get a new fix, plot a new course to your destination.

Always be very skeptical of your readings. When you get a fix, look around carefully and see if it makes sense. Is that buoy really where it says it should be? Is that point of land the same as your fix?

Keep taking bearings and question where you are at all times, because you never know what might crop up ahead—fog might roll in, or poor visibility and bad weather might hit. With these simple basics, you can figure out where you are, how long it took to get there, plot a new course to where you want to go, and estimate how much time it will probably take.

But there are other factors to consider when you're sailing along a coast, like figuring out any dangerous areas you need to avoid. For example, you might be sailing in waters with few hazards, and suddenly there's a large rock or reef you need to avoid. If you circle the rock in advance, it will catch your attention early and you can plan your route accordingly.

There's a lot more to learn than the basics you just went through. Take the time to study this important aspect of sailing and truly sail with confidence, wherever you are.

TIDES AND CURRENTS

Tides and currents are an important aspect of navigation. The U.S. government prints a constantly updated book called *Tidal Current Tables*. It covers twelve bodies of water on the East and West coasts. These tables give the maximum *flood* (incoming or rising tide) and *ebb* (period of tide between rising high water and succeeding low water), which cause currents. They also give the times these currents change direction. Some charts also show current direction with small arrows.

Current speed is called *drift*, and the direction of its flow is its *set*. Some navigators plot a course without allowing for current, and they plot another line that shows the boat's estimated path that allows for set and drift.

When you sail in areas of appreciable current, you must allow for its effects. Knowing the tides and currents in the area you are sailing in is a big part of knowing how to sail. When you're sailing in deep water over a long period of time, tides are not really a factor. But most of us sail close to land and go in and out of anchorages and harbors where tide levels become important. In some parts of the world, such as the coast of England, tide levels are so drastic (30 feet or more) that your boat can be sitting on flats hundreds of feet from the shore at low tide! In the United States, tides are not as dramatic. However, 2 or 3 feet can determine when and where you go in and out of channels and how you tie your boat to a dock. It's important to not only learn to read tables and charts, but to learn to read the water: know where silting occurs because of tidal movements; know the positions of reefs or rocks that pose a threat at low tide.

Tidal changes can be very regular and predictable in some areas of the country and erratic in others. Growing up in Maryland and then New York, I learned that tides went up and down at pretty much the same level, given the time of year, and always twice a day. On the Gulf Coast of Florida, where shallow waters prevail, there might be one tide a day or no tidal change in a 24-hour period. Sometimes, the change is a couple of inches, while at other times it's a couple of feet. Before you go out, check your weather station or local newspaper, which are both good sources for tidal information.

If you keep your boat at anchor, tide levels become important because they change the depth of the water under your keel. It's not only embarrassing, it's very uncomfortable to go aground at anchor. If you anchor in low tide—with just enough scope for that amount of water—and the tide comes in, you probably won't have enough anchor rode out at high tide to insure against dragging. The anchor is still on the bottom. But the angle the line makes is too sharp, and the anchor isn't able to dig in and hold. If you anchor in high tide with a lot of scope out and the tide goes out, you might find yourself either high and dry or dangerously close to a shoal area. It's easy to avoid both these situations: let more line out as the tide comes in, and tighten up on your rode as the tide goes out (assuming you are awake when either happens). In questionable situations at night, good sailors will have someone awake on anchor watch.

If you keep your boat at a fixed dock, which doesn't float up and down with the tide, you need to know how much the height of the water changes so you can leave your boat tied up properly. If your lines are too tight, the boat will be hanging from them rather than floating easily in the water at low tide. Also, there is the possibility of a line breaking or a cleat pulling out from this stress. If the lines are too loose, though not as much of a problem, you might find your boat floating far away from the dock and rubbing up against a piling or another boat that wasn't even close when you left the night before.

Current also affects where you sail. You've probably heard the old phrase, "still waters run deep." Not so. There is less current in shallow water (often along the shore) and more in deep water. For example, if you're racing and the current is against you, you'll want to get in close to shore where the current has less effect. If you're cruising, you still want to get out of strong current when it's against you—as long as there's enough water where the current is apt to be less. Sometimes you'll see a boat with sails perfectly set, but the boat appears to be standing still against the horizon. It could be aground. But it's more likely the boat is in current stronger than the wind and making no forward progress. It might even be going backwards.

Current direction depends on the tides. There are two channels in and out of Long Island Sound called the Race and the Gut. The current runs so fast here that sailors plan to leave the Sound on the outgoing current and return when it's flowing in. The water runs fast there because it's forced through a constricted area, like the stream created when you put your thumb partly over the nozzle of a hose.

If the wind is light and the current strong, the current is the dominant force in deciding where you sail. If the wind is strong and the current is strong, you have a better chance of getting where you want to go, though slower than if current were not a factor.

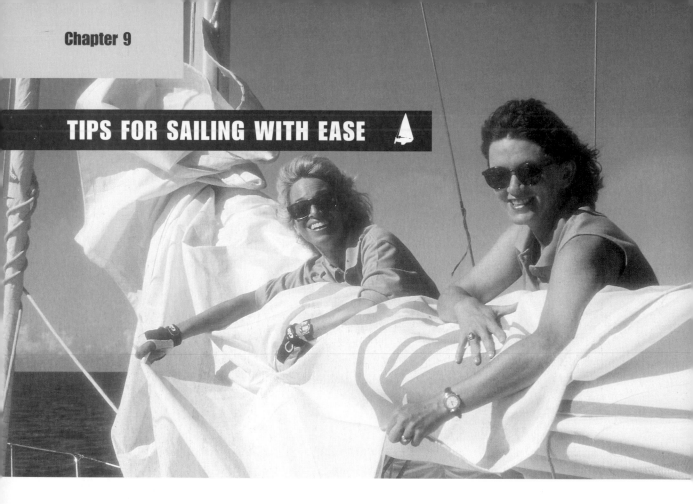

Chapter 9

TIPS FOR SAILING WITH EASE

It's time to set sail and use everything you've learned so far. This chapter includes drills you and your crew can practice to make your sailing smoother, exercises to make your body better prepared to perform onboard, and a host of different ideas for sailing on.

PRACTICE, PRACTICE, PRACTICE

Good sailors don't get good without practice. Now that you've learned the basic maneuvers in sailing, go out and practice until they become second nature. Before long you, your crew, and the boat will be moving in harmony. Don't let each crewmember keep the same position over and over. Change places after a series of maneuvers and do them again. Here are some exercises to help you work together as a team and hone your skills:

- **Trim for course changes.** Sail in a circle and go through the points of sail: from close-hauled, to a close reach, beam reach, broad reach, dead downwind; then jibe and sail up to a broad reach, beam reach, close reach, and close-hauled again. Repeat the circle in a counterclockwise direction. Keep your eyes on the telltales and adjust your sails properly for each point of sail.

- **Tack without losing speed.** Tack back and forth as you head upwind, over and over, at least fifteen times. As soon as you settle down with the boat moving on starboard tack, call for a tack to port, and vice versa. Do this until the time it takes to bring the jib in is minimum and each tack is as smooth as the next.

- **Shorten sail against the clock.** Practice reefing the mainsail. Time how long it takes and try to log a better time with each attempt.

- **Steer with just your sails.** Tie the helm down amidships, and sail the boat without it. Make sure you aren't around other boats, then move completely away from the tiller or wheel and make the boat go through the points of sail by trimming and easing the sails. (Steering with sails alone was reviewed in Chapter 5, page 85.)

- **Get out of irons.** Point the boat straight into the wind until it stops. Then practice backing the jib to get back under-

Top and above: Practice steering and trimming.

way. Do the same exercise again; but this time, push the mainsail out instead of the jib and make the boat move backward. Steer while you do this and gain confidence in helming the boat as it backs up.

- **Overboard recovery drills.** When no one is looking, throw a flotation pillow over the side and call, "Crew overboard!" Then go through the Quick Stop method (as described in Chapter 5, page 92). Take turns on the helm, and let everyone have a chance to do the pick-up. Practice the LifeSling method too, even if your boat doesn't have a LifeSling. Go through the maneuvers, pretend-

Top: Practice navigating under way. **Above:** Practice in heavy air: Betsy Alison at helm with her team.

ing the LifeSling is dragging behind you; or tie a long rope to your stern with a pillow attached to the end.

- **Controlled jibes.** Practice jibing. First do a dead downwind jibe with a controlled mainsheet, then do a reach-to-reach jibe, as described in Chapter 5. Take note of how long it takes you to bring the mainsail to centerline.

- **Chart and follow a course.** Practice navigation skills. Pick a destination that's out of sight. Now, chart a compass course to that point and steer that course. Figure out how much time it should take you to get there; check this time against your actual time. Take bearings and plot these on the chart. Are you where it says you are?

- **Practice docking.** Practice docking under sail (no engines). Decide in advance how wind and current will affect your approach and how you should be tied up when you finish. Then go through the maneuvers, using docklines and springlines. If your boat has an engine, practice the same exercise using the engine.

- **Practice anchoring.** Decide where you want to anchor. Determine the depth of the water and how much scope you'll need. Do this under sail and with an engine (if you have one). Let everyone take turns handling the helm and the anchor.

- **Get comfortable in more wind.** At first, do these exercises when the breeze is gentle and sailing is comfortable. But to really get good, do them when the wind is blowing hard and the seas kick up. Practice all the points of sail. Practice shortening sail. Do this in a controlled environment close to home and on a boat with crew you know.

  Of course, I'm not talking about going out in a hurricane or putting yourselves in danger. I'm talking about exciting conditions that get your adrenaline flowing—when the wind blows the tops off the waves, not much more than 25 knots. Why do this? Sooner or later, you're going to be out there when a storm hits. When it does, you know you'll be in control.

EXERCISES FOR SAILING

One of the wonderful things about sailing is how forgiving it is. You can participate at any exertion level—casual cruiser or hot racer. But during a course, you will do more drills and maneuvers in a short period of time than you would during a normal sailing outing. Chances are you'll discover a few new muscles and experience a different kind of fatigue at the end of each day. And you might feel like like Deborah Loeff—a pediatric surgeon in Chicago who bought her own boat—after her first lesson. "I loved it," she exclaimed. "Very athletic and mentally challenging."

Racing and sailing in small boats can provide quite an aerobic workout.

If you're overweight and out of shape, don't let this hold you back. You might run out of breath pulling lines, and you might feel clumsy getting around the boat at first. But the fact is, it won't hinder your ability to learn to sail. (However, you might want to think about starting a fitness program when you get home.) Certified instructors are trained to watch for signs of weariness and give you easier jobs or let you rest.

Sailors who race on a regular basis put their bodies through more extremes than casual sailors do, so they need to do more physical preparation. The 1995 all-women America's Cup team was up at 5 A.M.—running, bench pressing, and developing muscles that matched those of the male team members on other boats. But that's the extreme.

Women who sail regularly generally emphasize working on upper-body strength and toning. To compensate for small size or too little strength, Stephanie Argyris recommends learning to use your whole body—your trunk and hips, not just your arms.

Toning your body

While researching this book, I was surprised to find that few women thought about physical preparation before taking a sailing course. Maybe that's because fitness is so much a part of our daily lives. If you don't have a regular exercise regime, I suggest you do a little preparation each day to keep the minor aches at bay. These exercises can be done wherever you are—at home, on the road, in the gym—but they might not be for everyone. Check with your doctor, physical therapist, or trainer. Get a copy of *Fitness Afloat*, a video developed for sailors. Start slowly if you haven't exercised in a while.

- **Agility and suppleness.** Limber up before you go out. Bicycle 5 miles at a good, steady pace on a nice cool morning; use a stationary bike in the gym or at home; do a 20-minute fast walk. Stretch each morning to avoid a pulled muscle or soreness at the end of the day. The following exercises should be done in slow rhythmic repetitions, not sporadic pulsing, always with a flat back and tight stomach and buttocks. Take deep breaths throughout.

1.   While sitting on the floor, with legs wide apart in front, bend as far forward as you can.

2.   Still on the floor with legs still apart; twist, then stretch low over the right leg, then the left.

3.   Standing with feet shoulder-width apart, reach as high as you can, over and over.

4.   Standing, with arms straight out to your sides, twist at your waist as far as you can to one side, then the other.

5.   With your right arm over your head, your left hand on your hip, lean as far to left as you can. Then reverse.

6.   Relax your neck and lower shoulders. Keep your hands relaxed at your sides. Now rotate your head slowly down, to the right, to the back, around to the left, and to the front. Reverse and repeat.

- **Strengthen stomach muscles to avoid back stress.** The number of repetitions depends on your stamina. Start with eight of each and build up from there. Keep your back flat on the floor, knees bent, lower legs parallel to floor, stomach muscles and buttocks tight. Alternate flexed ankles with pointed toes to work the muscles in your lower legs.

1.   Put your hands behind your head, with elbows straight out to the sides, and lift your head up.

2.   Put your hands behind your head, with elbows straight out to the sides, and lift your upper body, then lower it.

3.   For these abdominal curls, put your arms straight out behind your head. Raise your upper body and your knees to your chest. Simultaneously bring your arms straight forward, outside your knees.

4.   For these elbow-to-knee abdominal curls, keep your feet off floor, your arms behind your head with elbows straight out to sides. Curl forward and bring your left elbow to right knee, then right elbow to left knee.

- **Arms and upper body.** When you do standing exercises, remember to keep your back and shoulders in line, buttocks tucked in, and stomach muscles tight. Legs should not be more than shoulder-width apart.

1. In a standing position, with legs shoulder-width apart, hold your upper arms against body, clench your fists, and raise your lower arms up and down from a fully extended position to as tightly bent an elbow as possible.

2. Lean forward from your waist with your back flat. Bring your arms tight to your sides and bend your elbows so your lower arms are tight against your upper arms. Tighten your arm muscles, extend your lower arms back, then forward again to closed elbow position. Repeat. Try this with small weights in your hands too.

3. Squeeze a tennis ball in each hand repetitively.

4. Using small weights or soup cans, extend your arms and roll your wrists.

- **Upper body and chest muscles.** Holding small weights or soup cans will augment these exercises. Always keep your back straight, and your stomach and buttock muscles tight.

1. With your arms straight out to your sides, at shoulder height, bend your elbows and keep your lower arms straight, so your arms make an **L**-shape. Bring your arms across chest until your hands and forearms meet. Return to your starting position. Repeat.

2. With your arms straight out to your sides at shoulder height, palms open and facing down, bring your arms across your chest and each other fully extended; pulse two times. Stretch arms back to starting position fully extended; turn palms away and pulse two times back as if you were pushing against a wall. Repeat.

- **Leg muscles.** Remember: For all the leg exercises, keep your buttocks tight (you get a little boost in shaping that area too), back straight, and stomach muscles tensed.

1. On the floor on your back, raise your buttocks and legs straight up. Support your lower back with your hands. Pump your legs fast, as if bicycling; alternate pointed toe and flexed ankles.

2. Standing facing a chair, door, or rail, hold onto the chair back, door knob, or rail with both hands. Raise your outside leg in front of you, with thigh as close to a right angle with the floor as possible, your knee bent, and your leg hanging straight down. Keeping this position, open your hip, and move your leg as far to your side as possible without twisting at the waist. Holding this position, extend your lower leg straight

out, then bring it back to a bent position. Alternate pointed toes and flexed foot. Repeat. Change sides and work your other leg.

3.   Facing a chair back or a rail, hold on with both hands, tighten your legs, raise yourself up on your toes, and lower yourself down several times.

Exercises aboard

Diana Smith, an avid racer and NWSA founding member, carries a 6-foot length of ¾-inch surgical tubing wherever she goes. On a boat, she hangs it over the boom or over handholds in the cabin below and pulls against it to strengthen her shoulders and upper back. For a simulated pectoral machine, she wraps it around a vertical post and sits with her back to the post, pulling the ends to the front. To simulate a rowing machine, she sits with feet extended and wraps the tubing around her soles.

Women who cruise over long distances find their bodies become sinewy and strong. They tend to eat less and consume healthier food. With no real deadlines, stress levels fade away; you feel younger and better. There are all kinds of exercises you can do when cruising, using various parts of the boat—the boom and handholds for stretching; bungee cords, winch handles, halyards and lines for upper body; foredeck surface and cockpit seats for leg work and abdominals. Cans of food work well as weights. The day-to-day activity of cruising is a workout in itself. You tense and relax muscles as you balance against the boat's movements, bend and pull on lines, row dinghies, and swim.

PERSONAL MATTERS

Now and then, women have to contend with situations that are less than wonderful on a boat. But if you come prepared, they are no big deal.

Sailing with your period

Some women sailors, myself included, have experienced sailing with fibroids and heavy bleeding. We didn't let that stop us. Wear extra protection on smaller boats, where there's nowhere to go to change, and make sure in advance you know approximately when you'll be getting back to shore. On a cruising boat, bring extra protection along and excuse yourself to go below and change when necessary. If you're a guest onboard, it's good etiquette to take your own waste away. Bring Ziploc bags for used tampons or pads, and opaque bags to take the Ziplocs off the boat. Never flush these down the boat's marine toilet: they will clog the system.

Going to the bathroom

No toilet on the boat? It's no big deal for a guy to go to the downwind side of the boat and pee. I used to hold it until it hurt. Now I always have a disposable cup and some tissue in my duffel. If I can't wait, I ask everyone else to turn the other way, and I pee as discreetly as possible. Then I rinse the cup overboard and stow it away in a Ziploc bag with the tissue. I haven't tried it, but some women carry a Freshette handheld urinary device with a tube attached to a small cup. If it's warm enough—providing you won't cause any delays if you're racing, and you can get back aboard easily—consider going for a swim to relieve yourself.

If there's a marine toilet (called a *head*) aboard, you're in luck. But be sure you know how to operate it before you sit down. Don't be shy. If there are no directions posted, ask someone on the boat about its operation.

Marine toilets discharge into a holding tank (some discharge overboard in some areas). They take in outside raw water to flush; when they're not in use, a lever on a hose leading to the bowl keeps that valve closed. When the valve is in line with the hose, it's open; when it's across the hose, it's closed. Before you sit down, open that valve to allow water in. If there's another lever on the toilet that points to *flush*, flip it to flush and pump the handle about six times to put water into the bowl. When finished, pump the handle at least fifteen times (twenty is better) to flush out the system. Then close the flush lever, pump the remaining water out until the bowl is dry, and close the hose valve. If you don't close all the valves, water can seep into the boat while you're sailing. Don't ever put anything down the toilet except toilet paper—and use this sparingly. Marine toilets are very sensitive, and they do not all operate alike. Sometimes there's a foot pedal. If you use the sink, you might have to open and close valves here too.

If you're pregnant

Your comfort level aboard will depend on how big you are, and whether or not you are prone to morning sickness. In the latter case, you probably won't want to go out for long—unless the winds are light and the water is calm. If you sail small boats that tip over, at some point getting back aboard is going to outweigh the fun of sailing. Pregnant sailors seem to sail as long as it's comfortable for them. Some even bear children while living aboard and cruising around the world. If the boat is a decent size, you won't have any trouble getting on or off. And if it has accommodations below, you can always stretch out for a rest.

After-sail care

After an exhilarating day of sailing, you're probably a little wet and gritty—especially if you sail on salt water. To freshen up, keep a towel, a change of clothes, cosmetics, and a hair dryer in your car trunk or in a locker ashore. Most marinas have showers. Diana Smith, who spends most weekend days racing on the Great Lakes and socializing in the club afterwards, says her all-time favorite piece of look-good equipment is her butane-fired curling iron. Conair and Braun both make these. She also carries a small 12-volt hair dryer made by ACAR she found at a powerboat accessory store that plugs into a cigarette lighter-type socket found on many cruising boats.

Sailing for the physically impaired

There's something magical about sailing, something that frees the spirit of the impaired. Shake-A-Leg and other organizations use specially rigged boats that allow a paraplegic to slide comfortably into the driver's seat and sail away from the dock. We taught an adult with cerebral palsy to sail on training boats without special gear. The old saying, "where there's a will, there's a way," works in spades for sailing. And the therapeutic qualities are invaluable. Don't let any physical impairment stop you from trying sailing. (See the Resource Directory for sources on special courses.)

KEEP ON SAILING

Women take to sailing because it suits a multitude of life designs—from occasional weekend outings, to weekly races or day sails, to the ultimate escape of cruising. Sailing is as appealing to women who excel in sports as it is to women who don't.

More and more women of all ages are gravitating to sailing as a vacation opportunity. Charter companies and groups around the world organize sailing events specifically designed to bring singles and couples together—to share the costs and experiences of exploring new territories, or to learn from the experts.

Many women are discovering sailing as an exciting path to a new lifestyle, with opportunities to make friends and enjoy leisure time in uncomplicated social settings. Some women meet their spouses and partners through sailing. Still others form alliances that lead to buying a boat and sharing maintenance costs. Career women find sailing the perfect get-away, both challenging and relaxing.

The next step

There are many ways you can take the next step in sailing. Below are some of the ways to continue on.

- **Go to sailboat shows.** Sailboat shows are excellent not only for learning about sailing but for meeting other sailors too. They run the gamut from small regional shows to major national events. Sailing schools, boat dealers, and product manufacturers and distributors exhibit at these shows. At some, free seminars and special programs are offered. You can even meet women sailing celebrities who inspire you to strike out on your own. Some of the bigger shows are well worth a weekend jaunt.

- **Go back to school.** After you learn the basics, you might want to continue your education and take a liveaboard cruising course, a performance sailing and racing course, or even a course on making long-distance ocean passages.

- **Tap into crew lists.** If you don't have a boat or plan to buy one, and if you don't have spare cash for some of the suggestions in this chapter, tap into crew lists available through commercial companies and computer bulletin boards, many of which are listed in the classified directories of sailing magazines. In various areas throughout the United States, there are women's sailing groups

A flotilla cruise raft-up.

with active sailing programs. Many focus on racing, which is a great way to improve your sailing.

- **Try flotilla cruising.** The easiest way to try cruising, with the least hassle and advance preparation, is to join one of the many flotilla cruises offered each year by sailing schools, charter companies, and sailing magazines. Designed for singles and couples who don't know anyone else to sail with (or lack the time to organize their own cruise), these unique vacations introduce avid sailors to new cruising grounds in one- or two-week adventures. A fleet of sailboats (the flotilla) sail on a set itinerary, led by a cruise leader and sometimes other experts who know the area well. Everyone shares the sailing, navigating, cooking, and having fun on boats that are generally 36 to 50 feet in length, with five or six participants on each. You don't have to go with a group: strangers sailing together for a week or two become a tight-knit group. Your sailing skill can be at any level. The organizers take responsibility for the boats. If there aren't enough experienced sailors in the group, they make sure someone is aboard who is qualified to take charge if need be. Your cost for everything (except airfare) can run from just under $1,000 for a week on the coast of Maine to over $2,000 for several weeks in the Greek islands.

● **Charter cruise with family and friends.** For families and friends ready to do a little exploring, this is a great vacation. When you charter, the boat is your hotel, you pack and unpack only once, see a different island or port every day, breathe fresh air, and swim in crystal waters.

You can rent a *bareboat*, which means you're in charge and there is no hired captain and crew. At least one person aboard (preferably more) have to be experienced sailors on a bareboat. Like the boats used for flotilla cruises, bareboats are fully equipped with all the supplies you need for comfortable cruising—linens and pillows for sleeping, complete galley supplies, navigation and safety equipment, tape decks and CD players, and all the food and drink you care to order in advance.

Bareboat operations can be found all over the world. In the Caribbean, high-season costs for a week run from just under $2,000 to over $6,000, depending on the size and type boat you charter. In the United States, one-week charters range from just over $1,000 to $4,000. Off-season discounts can be as much as 50 percent.

If you're not ready to bareboat, try a *crewed charter*. This is ultimate luxury (and more costly than bareboating). A knowledgeable captain, cook, and sometimes several crew (depending on the boat's size) handle the boat, the navigation, and all other preparations. You can take the helm and pull lines—but you won't have to do anything unless you want to.

Crewed charters like this one in the Caribbean can provide a marvelous way to relax with family and friends.

● **Rent a small or mid-sized boat.** You don't have to go far afield or spend a lot of money to keep on sailing. Nearly every marina in deep-water areas offers some form of sailboat rentals. If you have certification, but not a lot of experience, the people with the boats might still want to check you out. When you go on vacation, you'll find small-sailboat rentals by the hour or day right off the beach. Though they seldom ask about experience (figuring they'll just come and get you if you get into trouble), a real plus for you is having the knowledge to enjoy sailing fun the right way.

● **Explore sailing clubs.** Sailing clubs are popping up all over, and many are affiliated with sailing schools. The Offshore Sailing Club and Manhattan Yacht

Club both offer memberships for daysailing in New York Harbor. San Francisco Bay's Club Nautique, The Moorings in St. Petersburg, Florida, and the Chicago Sailing Club on Lake Michigan do the same. When you take a course, check with the school to see if they either have their own club or can hook you up with a club in the area. Private yacht and sailing clubs seem, on the surface, harder to join. In truth, some are quite exclusive. But many are looking to expand and offer social memberships to those who don't own boats. Some encourage you to post your name on their bulletin board as available crew. Don't be bashful. Ask to see the secretary at the club and find out what it takes to become a member.

> "**O**n vacation with two young children, we flew over the Rockies in a single-engine Cessna. I remember pointing to forests, telling the children how great the pine trees smell . . . then I realized that the scenery was about as real for them as a *National Geographic* TV special. . . . It would be a decade before they could take part in the excitement of flying. The following spring we switched to a 13-foot sailboat. Both children became accomplished sailors."
>
> —Marcia Andrews, age 60

- **Peruse the publications.** Opportunities for more sailing are advertised and reviewed in many sailing publications available on newsstands, including *Cruising World, Sail, Sailing, Sailing World,* and *Yachting.* The *Women's Sailing Resource,* published by the Women's Sailing Foundation, is full of ways to expand your sailing horizons.

To own a boat, or not to own

What does it take to own a sailboat? Costs of ownership will vary, depending on the boat's size, where you want to sail and berth it (dock versus mooring), and how much maintenance the boat requires. Older, wooden boats require more care and maintenance. But most old boats now are made of fiberglass, with far less cosmetic needs than wood. Small, off-the-beach boats are easy to trail around and lots of fun—with practically no maintenance requirements. Larger daysailers (a boat like a Colgate 26) are pretty maintenance free.

As you get into pocket cruisers with accommodations, engines, and electronics, the work list gets longer. But the trade-off is significant. There's just nothing better than setting sail for a weekend or even longer, leaving day-to-day routines on the dock, taking off with just the wind to guide you.

SOCIETY ONBOARD

Sailing with children can be rewarding and provide them with a life-long interest.

Sailing is not like tennis, where you need at least two people of well-matched skill to play. You can sail with any combination of people, each of whom are at different skill levels. You can even choose to sail alone.

You can invite your friends to discover your new love. To make it a good experience for them, start on days when you know the weather is going to treat you well, and find out if anyone is prone to seasickness. (Have a supply of wrist bands aboard just in case.) Suggest what to wear for comfort and safety. Keep some inexpensive foul-weather jackets aboard for your guests. Stop for lunch in a quiet cove instead of eating underway. Let them get the feel of the helm and encourage everyone to steer. When they're hooked, suggest you all go down to the Caribbean over the holidays and share a charter in paradise!

Mary Harper sailed a 1,700-mile solo passage across the Atlantic, from Newfoundland to Ireland, in her 30-foot sloop. At 79, this great-grandmother was the oldest person to cross the Atlantic alone. Several years earlier, she took an Offshore Sailing School course because she wanted to get involved in sailing again after her husband had died. Sailing helped her to reestablish her independence—in spades. On some trips, she takes crew along. But, "The trouble with male crew," she says, "is that they tighten everything so much you can't loosen it." To compensate for lack of strength, she has thoughtfully outfitted her boat for easier mechanical advantage, yet she keeps it simple enough to

handle on her own. Now well into her eighties, she sails singlehanded on her own boat, joins flotilla cruises in foreign ports, and preaches sailing to anyone who will listen.

Families form a special bond through sailing—often bringing rebellious teens and harried parents together in greater understanding of what's out there beyond television, school, and social pressures. But many women worry about how to make sailing safe when their children are aboard.

Kids take to sailing like they take to water, but you can use harnesses and netting to keep little ones aboard. Life vests are made for all sizes. Enroll your children in a club or community sailing program where they can learn on small, centerboard boats.

Cruising families get into home-schooling routines. Some have televisions, but most don't. They rely on books they swap with other cruisers, nature, and the people and places they visit for education and entertainment. The world is their backyard, the ocean their swimming pool. The Neales describe all this in the book, *All In the Same Boat.*

If you start your children at a young age, chances are you'll enjoy many quality hours on the water together as they grow up. But your girls might need special attention. Many who start avidly in youth club programs drop out in their teens. Some say it's the "boy thing," but I think it's the same old reason women lose interest: not enough stimulation, not being treated as equals with equal responsibility and respect.

There are some people, however, you want to avoid sailing with. Most men and women who scream on boats, call them screamers, are usually insecure sailors. The tenser the situation, the less confidence they have in themselves and everyone else—so they start barking orders and grabbing lines (especially lines others are holding). Don't waste time with the wrong sailing mates just because you love to sail.

. . . .

"Don't force your love for sailing on others. Just get away when you can and do it with people who are willing crew and enjoy the experience—people who you can spend many hours with in close quarters."

—Denise Theri, age 44

. . . .

When looking for a boat, here are some tips from Mimi Starke and other women who've gone through this exercise:

- First, find yourself a boat you believe in—one that's safe and relatively easy to handle in all conditions.

- If you're buying a used boat, have it surveyed for structural problems, ask who owned it and where they sailed, look at the sails and replace them if need be, have someone check the rigging or do it yourself.

- If it's a new boat, ask what it was designed for— light air, inland waters, oceangoing conditions? Sailing magazines do a lot of the groundwork for you in monthly reviews. When you narrow it down, call their editorial departments for reprints of the appropriate reviews.

- Talk to others who own the same make or type of boat. Find out where they sail, what their intentions are.

- Go out for a test sail, put the boat through its paces. See if you like the way it responds—particularly when it heels.

In recent years, boat partnerships have cropped up, with women sharing ownership and costs of maintaining and berthing a sailboat. How do you meet a potential co-owner? Through those flotilla cruises, Internet chat rooms, classified ads, sailing school courses, newsletters, and clubs.

CRUISING GEAR

. . . .

You don't need much for a cruise in warm waters. Here's what I pack for one week in warm, sunny weather—all in a carry-on duffel.

- Clothing and accessories: one pareo, a spare bra and six pairs of panties, one oversize T-shirt for sleeping, two pairs of shorts, one glamorous shore outfit, one outfit to lounge in, two bathing suits and cover-ups, hair accessories, minimal fun jewelry (not silver, because it tarnishes quickly in salt air), one light jacket or sweatshirt, one pair of slacks, two short-sleeved T-shirts, one hat with lanyard, one fanny pack, one pair of sailing gloves, one pair of boat shoes, one pair of reef shoes, one pair of sandals.

- Toiletries: deodorant, toothbrush and paste, razor, shampoo and conditioner, liquid soap or shampoo, skin lotion, water-proof mascara, lip balm and lipstick, medication and vitamins, tweezers and mirror, nail clips and file, hair brush and/or comb.

- Miscellaneous musts: camera, film and lens cleaner, regular eyeglasses and sunglasses

(continued on page 160)

CRUISING GEAR
● ● ● ● ● ● ● ● ● ● ● ● ● ● ● ● ● ● ● ●

(continued from page 159)

with cord, sunscreen, air tickets, cash, travelers checks and credit card, proof of ID (your passport is best) if traveling outside the United States.

- Optional items: hand-bearing compass, binoculars, paperbacks, cassette tapes or CDs, cooking spices, beach towel, Ziploc bags in assorted sizes, extra tote or duffel for souvenirs, small diary, snorkel and mask, can insulator, foul-weather gear jacket.

If your cruise takes you to the coast of Maine or to another cool region, take out the obvious Caribbean gear in the list above and add a full foul-weather suit, a fleece vest, a long-sleeved turtleneck top, sweater or sweatshirt, khaki pants, warm hat, and socks.

The thrill of racing is captured by these high fives after a race.

Racing or cruising?

About a third of the women who learn to sail gravitate to racing. Two-thirds of the women who teach sailing prefer racing to cruising, or they enjoy both equally. Racing keeps you on your toes, makes you think and plan ahead, and most instructors believe you learn more and sail better in competition: the greater the challenge, the steeper the learning curve.

If you want to get into racing, start reading the sailing magazines, attend seminars at yacht clubs and boat shows, and show up at the dock when you know there's a regatta. The most important things you can offer to a racing skipper are time and enthusiasm. If you can commit to the season's full schedule, you have a better chance of being invited into the crew. If you're willing to do whatever is needed, and focus on learning as much as you can about the various positions on the boat, you'll be asked to stay.

What do skippers look for in good crew? Vicki Sodaro, an active racer and coach who co-owns Hood Sailmakers in San Francisco, looks for crew who: wear proper attire and don't bring a lot of extra gear; don't talk a good story, just pitch in; do the job quietly without grumbling.

You should be discerning too. Check out the boat and skipper. Vicki says to look for someone who doesn't yell, assigns positions and tasks, and provides good food! The boat should exhibit good general maintenance with unfrayed lines, sails dry and folded, no frozen sheaves, no wire burrs.

If racing's not your bag, there are plenty of folks with cruising boats who would love to have the companionship of a skilled crew.

Lyn Fontanella, a founding board member of NWSA, will probably never own a sailboat. A dynamic New York City investment counselor in her fifties, she sails regularly with men and women she's met over the years. She's in great demand because she not only loves to sail, she's very helpful aboard.

Go sailing, however you choose to do it. The opportunities are endless, the life experiences unparalleled. You'll discover a new world—and a new you!

> "The competition [of sailboat racing] charges me up."
>
> —Kim Auburn, age 39

Chapter 10

RESOURCES

Many schools, publications, books, women's networking groups, and a host of learning opportunities for women will get you more involved in sailing. As founder and president of the Women's Sailing Foundation and its membership arm, the National Women's Sailing Association (NWSA), I find the list expanding monthly. You might want to get a copy of our *Women's Sailing Resource*, now in its third edition. But there are many other sources to help you satisfy your new passion and learn more about sailing. The most complete guides I've found are listed below. Sample some of these offerings and, through them, continue to expand your sailing horizons.

OTHER SOURCE BOOKS

These publications list just about anything and everything in sailing and are updated annually.

Sailboat Buyers Guide published by *SAIL* Magazine, 84 State Street, Boston, MA 02109-2202. Phone 800-362-8433; also available on CD-ROM and the web: www.sailbuyersguide.com

The Sailor's Sourcebook published by Miller Sports Group LLC, 5 John Clarke Rd., Box 3400, Newport, RI 02840-0992. Phone 800-634-1953; also on CD-ROM and the web: www.cruisingworld.com

Women's Sailing Resource published by the Women's Sailing Foundation, 16731 McGregor Blvd., Ft. Myers, FL 33908. Phone 800-566-6972; Fax 941-454-5859; E-mail: wsf@womensailing.org

BOOKS AND VIDEOS

Some very special catalogs, websites, and stores focus exclusively on sailing and marine activities. You'll find the books I recommend at these sources, along with a whole lot more.

Other how-to books on sailing

Bareboat Cruising by Diana Jessie, Tom Cunliffe, Shimon-Craig Van Collie, Chuck Place, Kim Downing, Rob Eckhardt, U.S. SAILING Certification Series, United States Sailing Association, 1996

Basic Cruising, US SAILING Certification Series, United States Sailing Association, 1995

Basic Keelboat by Monk Henry, US SAILING Certification Series, United States Sailing Association, 1995

Coastal Navigation by Tom Cunliffe, US SAILING Certification Series, United States Sailing Association, 1996

Colgate's Basic Sailing by Steve Colgate, Offshore Sailing School, Ltd., Inc., 1991

Fundamentals of Sailing, Cruising and Racing by Steve Colgate, W. W. Norton & Co., 1996

Learn to Sail in a Weekend by John Driscoll, 1st American ed., Knopf, 1998

Performance Sailing by Steve Colgate, Offshore Sailing School, Ltd., Inc., 1993

Sailing Fundamentals by Gary Jobson, Fireside, 1998

Sailing for Dummies by J. J. Isler and Peter Isler, IDG Books Worldwide, 1997

Start Sailing Right! The National Standard for Quality Sailing Instruction by Derrick Fries, US SAILING Small Boat Certification Series, United States Sailing Association, 1997

Steve Colgate on Cruising by Steve Colgate, Offshore Sailing School, Ltd., Inc., 1995. 800-221-4326

Steve Colgate on Sailing by Steve Colgate, W. W. Norton & Co., 1991. 800-221-4326

The Glenans Manual of Sailing by Davison and Simpson (translators), David & Charles Publishers, 1995

The Handbook of Sailing by Bob Bond, Knopf, 1992

Seamanship, weather, the ocean

The Annapolis Book of Seamanship by John Rousmaniere, Simon & Schuster, 1989

Boater's Bowditch by Richard Hubbard, International Marine, 1997

Chapman Piloting: Seamanship and Small Boat Handling, 62nd edition, by Elbert S. Maloney and Charles Frederic Chapman, Hearst Books, 1996

Fire and Ice by Paul Garrison, Avon Books, 1998

Navigation Rules: International-Inland, Gordon Press, 1997

The Klutz Book of Knots: How to Tie the World's 25 Most Useful Hitches, Ties, Wraps, and Knots by John Cassidy, Klutz Press, 1985

Waves and Beaches by Willard Bascom, Doubleday, 1980. (Currently out of print.)

Women's experiences

Coming About: A Family Passage at Sea by Susan Tyler Hitchcock, Ballantine Books, 1998

Just Cruising by Liza Copeland, Romany Enterprises, 1993

Mahina Tiare: Pacific Passages by John Neal and Barbara Marrett, Pacific International Publishing Co., 1993

Maiden Voyage by Tania Aebi, Bernadette Brennan, reprint edition, Ballantine Books, 1996

Sonnet: One Woman's Voyage from Maryland to Greece by Lydia Bird, North Point Press, 1997

Still Cruising—A Family Travels the World: Australia to Asia, Africa and America by Liza Copeland, Romany Enterprises, 1996

Taking the Helm: One of America's Top Sailors Tells Her Story by Dawn Riley with Cynthia Flanagan, Little, Brown & Co., 1995

Advice from sailing experts

All in the Same Boat: Family Living Aboard and Cruising by Tom Neale, International Marine/McGraw-Hill, 1997

Cruising for Cowards: Strategies, Boats and Equipment Preferred by Experienced Cruisers by Liza Copeland, Romany Press, 1997

The Cruising Woman's Advisor: How to Prepare for the Voyaging Life by Diana Jessie, International Marine, 1997

Dragged Aboard: A Cruising Guide for the Reluctant Mate by Don Casey, W. W. Norton & Co., 1998

Sailors' Secrets: Advice from the Masters, edited by Michael Badham and Robby Robinson, International Marine/McGraw-Hill, 1997

The Voyager's Handbook: The Essential Guide to BlueWater Cruising by Beth Leonard, International Marine, 1998

Videos

Annapolis Book of Seamanship with John Rousmaniere: Daysailers, Sailing & Racing

Learn to Sail with Steve Colgate,
Offshore Sailing School
16731 McGregor Boulevard
Ft. Meyers, FL 33908
Phone 800-221-4326
E-mail: offshore@coconet.com
www.offshore-sailing.com

Fitness Afloat
Fitness Afloat Corporation
40 Elm St.
Newport, RI 02840
Phone 877-FIT-AFLOAT
www.fitnessafloat.com

Sailing Fundamentals with Peter Isler, 1996
American Sailing Association
13922 Marquesas Way
Marina del Rey, CA 90292
Phone 310-822-7171
Fax 310-822-4741
E-mail: info@american-sailing.com
www.american-sailing.com

Websites and catalogs for sailing books and videos

Armchair Sailor
543 Thames St.
Newport, RI 02840
Phone 800-29CHART
Fax 401-847-1219
www.seabooks.com

Bennett Marine Video, Inc.
3779 Cahuenga Boulevard West
Studio City, CA 91604-3405
Phone 800-733-8862
www.videoflicks.com/BMV/
  index.html

Bluewater Books & Charts
1481 SE 17th St.
Ft. Lauderdale, FL 33316
Phone 800-942-2583
Fax 954-522-2278
E-mail: help@bluewaterweb.com
www.bluewaterweb.com

Celestaire
416 S. Pershing
Wichita, KS 67218
Phone 800-727-9785
Fax 316-686-8926
E-mail: info@celestaire.com
www.celestaire.com

Complete Cruising Solutions
1813 Clement Ave., #24
Alameda, CA 94501
Phone 510-769-1547

Cruiser's Guide Videos
PO Box 591
Denver, CO 80201
Phone 800-232-8902

Cruising Guide Publications, Inc.
1130 B Pine Hurts Rd.
Dunedin, FL 34698
Phone 814-733-5322

International Marine Boating Books Catalog
The McGraw-Hill Companies
Customer Service Department
PO Box 547
Blacklick, OH 43005
Phone 800-262-4729

Landfall Navigation
354 West Putnam Ave.
Greenwich, CT 06830
Phone 203-661-3176

Nautical Mind/Marine Booksellers & Charts Agents
249 Queen's Quay West
Toronto, ON M5J 2N5 Canada
Phone 416-203-1163
Fax 416-203-0729
E-mail: books@nauticalmind.com
www.nauticalmind.com

Paradise Cay Publications
PO Box 29
Arcata, CA 95518-0029
Phone 800-736-4509

SailCo Press
PO Box 2099
Key Largo, FL 33037
Phone 305-743-0626

MAGAZINES

Canadian Yachting
395 Matheson Boulevard East
Mississauga, ON L4Z 2H2, Canada
Phone 905-890-1846
Fax 905-890-5769
E-mail: canyacht@kerrwil.com
www.canyacht.com

Cruising World
5 John Clarke Road, Box 3400
Newport, RI 02840-0992
Phone 401-847-1588
Fax 401-848-5048
www.cruisingworld.com

Latitude 38
15 Locust Avenue
Mill Valley, CA 94941
Phone 415-383-8200
Fax 415-383-5816
www.latitude38.com

Ocean Navigator
PO Box 569
Portland, ME 04112-0569
Phone 207-772-2466

SAIL Magazine
84 State Street
Boston, MA 02109
Phone 617-720-8600

Sailing Magazine
125 E. Main Street
Port Washington, WI 53074
Phone 414-284-3494,
www.sailnet.com

Sailing World
5 John Clarke Road, Box 3400
Newport, RI 02850-0992
Phone 401-847-1588
Fax 401-848-5048
www.sailingworld.com

Soundings
35 Pratt Street
Essex, CT 06426
860-767-3200
E-mail:
  soundings@traderonline.com
www.soundingspub.com

Southwinds
PO Box 1190
St. Petersburg, FL 33731
Phone 727-825-0433
Fax 727-898-2211
E-mail:
   editor@southwindssailing.com
www.southwindssailing.com

Spinsheet
301 Fourth Street
Annapolis, MD 21403
Phone 410-216-9309

Yachting Magazine
2 Park Avenue
New York, NY 10016
Phone 212-779-5300
www.yachtingmag.com

WOMEN'S NEWSLETTERS

Take the Helm, National Women's
   Sailing Association
16731 McGregor Boulevard
Ft. Myers, FL 33908
Phone 800-566-6972
Email: wsf@womensailing.org

SisterSail
c/o Paradise Cay
PO Box 29
Arcata, CA 95518-0029
Phone 800-736-4509

Women Aboard
2626 PGA Boulevard, #123
Palm Beach Gardens, FL 33410
Phone 561-775-4688
Fax 561-775-4687
www.sspboatsite.com/womenaboard

SAILING SCHOOLS AND SPECIAL LEARNING EVENTS

There are literally *thousands* of sailing
schools across the country and around
the world. A few schools specialize
exclusively in courses for women.
Most are coed, but some of these offer
special women's programs in addition
to regular schedules. Because the list
would take up this entire book, I suggest you check out the schools below
and consult the source books and
associations listed above for more.
Ask for brochures, talk to their repre-
sentatives, tell them what you want
. . . and demand the best. Many of
the instructors quoted in this book
and many others who provided
invaluable tips—all experienced and
certified—either teach on their own
or at one of the schools listed below.

Sailing school directories

**Canadian Yachting
   Association**
1600 James Naismith Drive
Gloucester, ON K1B 5N4 Canada
Phone 613-748-5687
Fax 613-748-5688
E-mail: SailCanada@sailing.ca
www.sailing.ca

**National Sailing Industry
   Association**
200 E. Randolph Dr.
Chicago, IL 60601-6528
Phone 800-535-SAIL

US SAILING
Box 1260
Portsmouth, RI 02871-0907
Phone 401-683-0800
Fax 401-683-0840
E-mail:ussailing@compuserv.com
www.ussailing.org

COED SCHOOLS

Annapolis Sailing School (Florida,
   Maryland, St. Croix)
601 6th Street
PO Box 3334
Annapolis, MD 21403
Phone 800-638-9192
Fax 410-268-3114
E-mail: annapway@clark.net
www.usboat.com/shows/bshomes.htm

Club Nautique (California)
Alameda
1150 Ballena Boulevard, suite 161
Alameda, CA 94501
Phone 800-343-SAIL

Sausalito
100 Gate Six Road
Sausalito, Ca 94965
Phone 800-559-CLUB
Fax 415-332-0740
E-mail:
   103115,3127@compuserve.com

Marina del Rey
13953 Panay Way
Marina del Rey, CA 90292
Phone 877-477-SAIL
www.sailors.com/clubnautique

J-World (Annapolis)
213 Eastern Avenue
Annapolis, MD 21403
Phone 800-966-2038
Fax 410-280-2079
E-mail: sailjwa@sailjworld.com
www.sailjworld.com

J-World (Newport, RI, and Key
   West, FL)
Phone 800-343-2255
Fax 401-849-8168
E-mail: jwrld@aol.com
www.paw.com/sail/jworld

J-World (San Diego)
Phone 800-666-1050
Fax 619-224-2468
E-mail: jworld@adnc.com
www.jworldsd.com

Offshore Sailing School (Florida,
   Caribbean, Rhode Island, New
   Jersey, New York, Connecticut,
   Illinois)
16731 McGregor Boulevard
Fort Meyers, FL 33908
Phone 800-221-4326
Fax 941-454-1191
E-mail: offshore@coconet.com
www.offshore-sailing.com

**OCSC–San Francisco Bay Sailing
   School**
1 Spinnaker Way
Berkeley, CA 94710
Phone 800-223-2984
Fax 510-843-2155
E-mail: info@ocsc-sfbay.com
www.sailors.com/ocsc

Orange Coast College Sailing Center
1801 West Pacific Coast Highway
Newport Beach, CA 92603
Phone 714-645-9412
Fax 714-645-1859
E-mail: kmiller@lib-occa.occ.edu
www.occsailing.com

Seacraft Sailing Academy
1019 Q Avenue, suite D
Anacortes, WA 98221
Phone 360-299-2526

WOMEN-ONLY COURSES

At the Helm Sailing School
Phone 281-334-4101
Fax 281-334-2840

Betsy Alison Race Clinics
Phone 401-848-5146

Offshore Sailing School
Phone 800-221-4326
Fax 941-454-1191
E-mail: offshore@coconet.com
www.offshore-sailing.com

Orange Coast College Adventure Sailing
Phone 714-645-9412
Fax 714-645-1859
E-mail: kmiller@lib-occa.occ.edu
www.occsailing.com

Sea Sense
PO Box 1961
St. Petersburg, FL 33731
Phone 800-332-1404
E-mail: seasense@aol.com
www.seasenseboating.com

Women's Sailing Adventures
39 Woodside Avenue
Westport, CT 06880
Phone 800-328-8053
Fax 203-227-7413
E-mail: 76521,235@compuserve

SPECIAL LEARNING EVENTS FOR WOMEN

Bitter End Yacht Club and Resort,
December women's week,
800-872-2392

Offshore Sailing School,
spring/summer women's weeks,
800-221-4326

Northern California Women's Sailing Seminar, March weekend,
510-881-5422

Take the Helm: Women's Weekends, hands-on workshops
and seminars, 800-566-6972

Tania Aebi's Adventures, periodic
sailing trips, 800-994-7245

Women's Sailing Convention
(Southern California), February
women's weekend, 714-730-1797

OTHER EVENTS

"GO SAILING!" annual nationwide
introductory sail weekend in July
sponsored by Sail America,
800-817-SAIL

SAILING PROGRAMS FOR THE PHYSICALLY CHALLENGED

All of these organizations offer special programs for a variety of physical conditions, some with specially
adapted boats, others adapting the
sailor to boats you and I sail on.

Disabled Sailing Association of British Columbia
1300 Discover
Vancouver, BC V6R 4L9, Canada
Phone 604-222-3003

National Ocean Access Project
Annapolis City Marina
Suite #306
410 Severn Avenue
Annapolis, MD 21403
Phone 410-268-0660

Sail-Habilitation
Dr. Stephanie Argyris
9 Hospital Drive
Toms River, NJ 08753
Phone 908-505-0202

Shake-a-Leg
PO Box 1002
Newport, RI 02840
Phone 401-782-6280

GENERAL OUTDOOR COURSES AND NETWORKING

Becoming an Outdoors-Woman
Dr. Christine Thomas
College of Natural Resources
University of Wisconsin–Stevens
  Point
Stevens Point, WI 54481
Phone 87-BOWOMAN
E-mail: cthomas@uwsp.edu
www1.uwsp.edu/general/commun/
  bow/index.htm

National Outdoor Leadership School
288 Main Street
Lander, WY 82520
Phone 307-332-6973
Phone for Leave No Trace
  800-332-4100
Fax 307-332-1220
E-mail: admissions@nols.edu
www.nols.edu/

Women's Outdoor Network
PO Box 50003
Palo Alto, CA 94303
Phone 650-494-8583
Fax 650-712-9093
E-mail: wonforfun@earthlink.net
home.earthlink.net/~wonforfun/

Women's Sports Foundation
Eisenhower Park
East Meadow, NY 11554
Phone 800-227-3988, 516-542-4700
Fax 516-542-4716
E-mail: wosport@aol.com
www.lifetimetv.com/WoSport

BOAT SHOWS

Regional boat shows are held in most
communities where there's water to
sail on. Check your local newspapers
for dates. For the ultimate experience,
I urge you to visit one of the shows

listed below. Check for dates and locations in the boat show calendars of sailing magazines. Many are in-the-water shows where free sailing rides and seminars are offered. You'll find the largest number and array of sailboats at the granddaddy of them all—the U.S. Sailboat Show in Annapolis. During winter months, you can get a refreshing "sailing fix" at the Chicago and Atlantic City shows, where an incredible variety of seminars are offered, including NWSA's "Take the Helm" series for women.

Newport International Boat Show, Newport, Rhode Island, in September

Pacific SAIL EXPO, Oakland, California, in April

SAIL EXPO, Atlantic City, New Jersey, in February and St. Petersburg, Florida, in November

Seattle International Boat Show, Seattle, Washington, in January

Strictly Sail, Chicago, Illinois, in January or February, and Hartford, Connecticut, in March

United States Sailboat Show, Annapolis, Maryland, in October

CREW LISTS

Some of the outfits listed below focus on job opportunities on sailboats and may charge a fee. Others provide a free service that help women meet up with other women and men looking for sailing companions.

Captains and Crew
5300 Longbay Road
St. Thomas, USVI 00802

Certified Crew Services
PO Box 707
Port Washington, NY 11050

Crew Unlimited
2065 S. Federal Hwy
Ft. Lauderdale, FL 33316
Phone 954-462-4624

Hassle Free Inc.
1550 SE 17th Street, suite 5
Ft. Lauderdale, FL 33316
Phone 954-763-1841

National Women's Sailing Association
16731 McGregor Blvd.
Ft. Myers, FL 33908
Phone 800-566-6972

Sea Sense
PO Box 467
Higganum, CT 06441
Phone 800-332-1404

NETWORKING OPPORTUNITIES

Here are the sailing groups and events I know about at this time, but new ones form every day as women around the country seek camaraderie among their sailing peers. Most of these associations hold annual racing regattas and events. For example, the Southern California Yachting Association has produced an annual Women's Sailing Convention organized by Gail Hine in February, with over 300 women attending each year since 1988. The NWSA "Take the Helm" program is available at many boat shows and other venues. When you hook up with one of these associations, you'll find yourself sailing, racing, and learning more from an enthusiastic group of very giving women.

Women's sailing associations

Chicago Women's Sailing Network, 312-321-4282

Florida Women's Sailing Association, 813-254-8125

Hawaii Women's Yacht Racing Association, 808-946-9061

Long Beach/Los Angeles Women's Sailing Association, 310-547-3929

Milwaukee Community Sailing Center, 414-277-9094

National Women's Sailing Association, 800-566-6972

North Coast (Cleveland) Women's Sailing Association, 216-526-7783

Northern California Women's Sailing Association, 510-881-5422

Seattle Women's Sailing Association, 206-298-2861

Southern California Yachting Association, 714-730-1797

Wet Hens (Hawaii), 800-879-9665

Windjammers of Clearwater, 813-585-6555

Women's Ocean Racing Sailing Association, 714-870-8009

Internet sites and chat rooms

More and more interest in sailing is appearing on-line. You can chat with thousands of sailing women around the world or find out about boats, gear, catalogs, schools, and places to go sailing on the web.

America Online
click "The Exchange" for "Sailing"

CompuServe Incorporated
click on "Sailing"

National Women's Sailing Association
www.sailnet.com/nwsa for an active chat room

Sailnet
www.sailnet.com

The Sailing Source
www.paw.com/sail

FLOTILLA CRUISES AND CHARTERS

The list of companies that charter sailboats with or without crew is long, covering just about any beautiful cruising area in the United States, the Caribbean . . . in fact, the world. Please pick up one of the resources listed earlier and check out all those fantastic destinations you can see under sail. A few of the companies and organizations that offer no-hassle sailing trips you can join as an individual are listed below. Ask to be on a boat with other women (and men) who share your desire to see the world under sail.

Cruising World Adventure Charters
See any issue of *Cruising World* magazine for upcoming trips, 401-847-1588

Offshore Cruising Club
Contact Offshore Sailing School for graduate flotilla cruises, 800-221-4326

Sailing Singles
164 South Main
Suite #421
Parkville, MO 64152
Phone 800-615-4006 for flotilla cruises

Sunsail
980 Awald Road, suite 302
Annapolis, MD 21403
Phone 800-327-2276

Sun Yacht Charters
PO Box 737
Camden, ME 04843
Phone 800-772-3500

The Moorings, Ltd.
Flotilla, bareboat, and crewed charters, 800-535-7289

SAILING CLUBS

Here are some commercial sailing clubs you can join and sail as often as you like. Check your yellow page directories for a community sailing center near you for more daysailing opportunities. Costs are low compared to owning a sailboat. Some commercial clubs require an initiation fee and modest annual dues, but no other requirements other than the ability to sail. Lacking that crucial ingredient, many will teach you first.

Chicago Sailing Club,
312-871-7245

Club Nautique,
800-343-SAIL (Alameda)
800-559-CLUB (Sausalito)
www.sailors.com/clubnautique

Manhattan Yacht Club
212-786-3323

Offshore Sailing Club
800-221-4326 (Captiva Island, FL;
New York Harbor, NY; Chicago,
IL; Stamford, CT)
www.offshore-sailing.com

GEAR FOR YOU

Many of these companies have stores, websites, and catalogs that cover a multitude of sailing desires and shapes. Some also carry gear for your boat and stuff to take along. Some have multiple locations across the States, so call to find the one nearest you. Spend a little time in a BOAT/U.S. or West Marine store (there are hundreds across the country) and get a feel for all the many products available to make sailing easier and more fun.

BOAT/U.S.
880 S. Pickett Street
Alexandria, VA 22304
Phone 800-937-2628
www.boatus.com

Commodore Uniform & Nautical Supplies
335 Lower County Road
Harwichport, MA 02646
Phone 800-438-8643

Davis Instruments
3465 Diablo Avenue
Hayward, CA 94545
Phone 800-678-3669

Defender Industries
321 Main Steet
New Rochelle, NY 10801
Phone 914-632-3001

Extrasport
5305 NW 35th Court
Miami, FL 33142
Phone 305-633-2945

Fawcett Boat Supplies
110 Compromise Street
Annapolis, MD 21401
Phone 410-267-8681
www.fawcettboat.com

Harken, Inc.
1251 E. Wisconsin Ave.
Pewaukee, WI 53072
Phone 414-691-3320

Helly Hansen (U.S.) Inc.
17275 NE 67th Court
Redmond, WA 98052-4952
Phone 425-883-8823
Fax 425-882-4932

Henri Lloyd
405 Main Street, unit 6
Port Washington, NY 11050
Phone 800-645-6516

JSI–The Sailing Source
3000 Gandy Boulevard
St. Petersburg, FL 33702-2045
Phone 800-234-3220
www.jsisail.com

High Seas/High Sierra/Sierra Sport
Phone 947-913-1100

Kokatat
5350 Ericson Way
Arcada, CA 95521
Phone 707-822-7621

Offshore Sailing Catalog
Phone 800-221-4326

Patagonia Mail Order
PO Box 32060
Reno, NV 89533
Phone 800-638-6464
www.patagonia.com

Stormy Seas, Inc.
PO Box 1570
Poulsbo, WA 98370
Phone 360-779-4439

Ultimate Products, Inc.
4893-D West Waters Avenue
Tampa, FL 33634
Phone 800-477-HATS

West Marine Products/E&B
  Supply
500 West Ridge Drive
Watsonville, CA 95076-4100
Phone 800-262-8042

Sun protection and specialty clothing for women

I just had to list some of these for you. Some offer only apparel and accessories. Others offer neat products to make sailing easier. And still others make or carry a potpourri of gear and gadgets for ultimate safety and sailing fun. I especially recommend you stop by Team One Newport (great for the guys you sail with, too). Ask for owner Martha MacKechnie if you get to that fantastic sailing mecca, or give them a shout on the web.

Capt. Al's Products, Inc.
PO Box 370153
West Hartford, CT 06137-0153
Phone 860-232-9065

Douglas Gill USA
6087 Holiday Road
Buford, GA 30518
Phone 770-945-0788
www.douglasgill.com

Helly Hansen (U.S.) Inc.
17275 NE 67th Court
Redmond, WA 98052-4952
Phone 425-883-8823
Fax 425-882-4932

Sailing Angles
4040 SW 60 Court
Miami, FL 33155
Phone 305-661-7200

Sun Precautions (Solumbra fabric)
2815 Wemore Avenue
Everett, WA 98201
Phone 800-882-7860
www.solumbra.com/shade

Team One Newport
PO Box 1443
547 Thames Street
Newport, RI 02840
Phone 800-VIP-GEAR
Fax 401-849-8460
www.team1newport.com
email: info@team1newport.com

Eye protection

Hobie Sunglasses
5866 South 194th Street
Kent, WA 98032
Phone 800-554-4335

Polaroid (Sunglass Division)
1 Upland Road., N-2
Norwood, MA 02062
Phone 800-225-2770

Serengeti Eyewear
203 Colonial Drive
Horseheads, NY 14845
Phone 800-525-4001

Solar-Mates
8125 25th Court East
Sarasota, FL 34243
Phone 800-426-7849
www.h2optix.com

Vuarnet-France Optical
5440 McConnel Avenue
Los Angeles, CA 90066
Phone 310-301-4966

Skin protection

There're tons of skin products on the market and I'm sure you have your favorites. I like Bull Frog, but a few other companies specialize in sailing and often exhibit at boat shows.

Chattem (Bull Frog)
1715 W. 38th Street
Chattanooga, TN 37409
Phone 800-233-3764

Nauti-Care
PO Box 636
Severna Park, MD 21146
Phone 800-262-0202

North Safety Products
  Health Care Division
1515 Elmwood Road.
Rockford, IL 62213
Phone 815-877-2531

Nautical jewelry

Most women sailors I know love to wear fine jewelry that speaks of sailing, the oceans, and magical sea creatures. The best nautical jeweler is Tony Correa, a loyal champion of women sailors. His jewelry is handmade and admired by all.

A.G.A. Correa & Son
Phone 800-341-0788

Medical supplies for sailing

The best book I've found for emergency medicine on the high seas is (believe it or not) *Medicine for Mountaineering*, published by The Mountaineers in Seattle, Washington. But a longtime doctor-sailor has made emergency care very easy with several different supply paks, accommodating all types and lengths of sailing outings and voyages.

Medical Seapak
1945 Ridge Road East, #105
Rochester, NY 14622
Phone 716-266-3136

Women's wellness

The Melpomene Institute
1010 University Avenue
St. Paul, MN 55104
Phone 612-642-1951
www.melpomene.org

Index